MORE STORIES
BEHIND THE BEST-LOVED
SONGS
of
CHRISTMAS

Other Books by Ace Collins

MORE STORIES
BEHIND THE BEST-LOVED
SONGS
of
CHRISTMAS

ACE COLLINS
BESTSELLING AUTHOR

ZONDERVAN®

GRAND RAPIDS, MICHIGAN 49530 USA

ZONDERVAN.COM/
AUTHORTRACKER

ZONDERVAN®

More Stories Behind the Best-Loved Songs of Christmas
Copyright © 2006 by Andrew Collins

Requests for information should be addressed to:

Zondervan, *Grand Rapids, Michigan 49530*

Library of Congress Cataloging-in-Publication Data

Collins, Ace
　　More stories behind the best-loved songs of Christmas /
Ace Collins.
　　　　p. cm.
　　ISBN-10: 0-310-26314-X
　　ISBN-13: 978-0-310-26314-2
　　1. Carols, English—History and criticism. 2. Popular
music—History and criticism. 3. Christmas music—History and
criticism. I. Title.
ML1400.C6　2006
264'.23—dc22

2006007198

This edition printed on acid-free paper.

Interior design by Michelle Espinoza

Printed in the United States of America

---

06 07 08 09 10 11 12 • 15 14 13 12 11 10 9 8 7 6 5 4 3 2 1

To Matthew Harless,
who during his brief time on earth
taught everyone who knew him
the true joy to be found in every moment of life

CONTENTS

INTRODUCTION

hen doing the first book in this series, *Stories Behind the Best-Loved Songs of Christmas*, I had as much fun as I have ever had with a writing project. In a sense, each day that I worked on that book, dug through research, and uncovered more facts behind the songs was like having one Christmas on top of another. At the time I finished, I had no idea if readers would come to appreciate the stories behind the songs, but I knew that each of those thirty-one chapters had deeply enriched my appreciation of the holidays.

Well, I soon found out that readers did want to know the stories behind Christmas carols. Because of the success of *Stories Behind the Best-Loved Songs of Christmas*, Zondervan asked me to research and write a book on holiday customs. *Stories Behind the Great Traditions of Christmas* allowed me again to experience the joy and spirit of Christmas, day after day for months at a time. Rather than being tired of Christmas when I concluded this project, I was so excited by knowing the stories behind both the carols and the customs that I couldn't wait for the next holiday season to begin.

I can't begin to explain how excited I was when Zondervan asked for a third book, this one telling the stories behind even more beloved Christmas songs. As I began to target another batch of seasonal carols and uncover their stories, I came to realize what an incredible gift my publisher had given me.

More Stories Behind the Best-Loved Songs of Christmas embraces the songs of classical history, folk music, and even modern country and jazz. In these pages, three of the famed

Albert Burt carols are spotlighted, and those stories will not just make your holidays brighter, they might forever change your life. When you know the stories behind the unforgettable moving Christmas tributes of writers as varied as Charles Wesley, Bill Gaither, Willie Nelson, and Skip Ewing, you may never look at the holidays the same way again.

Just as Christmas is like no other time, these stories of the carols allow each of us to go to a particular moment in time and be moved in ways that will bring Christ alive in our December thoughts, as well as in our actions. As you will find, in *More Stories Behind the Best-Loved Songs of Christmas* not only have we included many old favorites but we have had the chance to spotlight the wonderful stories behind a new generation of Christmas songs. So while you will probably gain a fresh appreciation of traditional fare such as "Ave Maria," "Carol of the Bells," Handel's "Hallelujah Chorus," and "Little Drummer Boy," you might also fall in love with relatively new offerings like "Christmas Shoes," "Come and See What's Happening in the Barn," "Merry Christmas, Darling," and "Thank God for Kids."

After the release of the first book in this series, I received many letters asking why we did not include the words to all of the songs in that book. Whenever we can, we do print the lyrics, but lyrics to songs written in the past seventy-five years are owned by the publishers of these works. Often there are rules which prevent the publication of those newer lyrics for use in books such as this. Yet even if the lyrics are not printed here, it is very easy to find them through published sheet music, on the websites of the many artists who have recorded these classics, or perhaps even in music books or on CD inserts that you already own. Besides, if you are like me, you probably already know most of the words to almost all of these wonderful holiday offerings.

One of the songs in this book is "If Every Day Was Like Christmas." Thanks to these assignments, so many of my days have become just like Christmas. I hope that when you read this book, more of your days will have the magic, the joy, the wonder, and the flavor of the most wonderful day of the year!

Handel's Hallelujah Chorus

he "Hallelujah Chorus" is arguably the most powerful piece of music ever written. Though its lyrics are sparse, its meaning is monumental. These powerful words, coupled with one of the most awe-inspiring pieces of music ever penned, put an unmistakably and unabashedly spiritual exclamation point on each Christmas season. This song now reverberates so strongly during the holidays that for many, Christmas does not begin until the "Hallelujah Chorus" has been performed. It is at that moment, when the first hallelujah is delivered and people rise as one to their feet, that the true meaning of Christ's birth is again joyously proclaimed by his people.

Yet there is an irony in the belief that it can't be Christmas without Handel's most famed composition. The song itself was never intended for a Christmas audience. It was originally considered to be an Easter offering. And, to make this story even more unbelievable, when he composed his most famous work, the great George Handel was a washed-up has-been, a frail forgotten man living in abject poverty. While penning what is now widely thought of as the world's most dynamic musical salute to the birth of the Savior, Handel essentially was reborn himself.

The great composer was born in Halle, Germany, on February 23, 1685. Though a gifted musician, Handel actually flunked out of college. Moving to Hamburg at eighteen, he began to write operas. He was only modestly successful there, so in 1706 he relocated to Italy. Inspired by the country's history, within three years a reenergized Handel composed two oratorios that were praised by both music critics and the public. Suddenly, George was a local star, the "king of the oratorios."

Few modern songwriters devote their talents to creating an oratorio, but Handel loved these sacred musicals. Oratorios were essentially dramatic musical presentations of biblical stories written for choruses but featuring strong soloists in the production's most important segments. Created to provide moral lessons along with classical entertainment, oratorios closely resembled opera without costumes or staging. Inexpensive to produce and easy to understand, the productions were popular with both common people and the elite. Most important to Handel, they offered him a chance to succeed while also reflecting his convictions.

Handel was a man of deep faith. He prayed often and studied his Bible. He believed that his talent and inspiration came from God. He saw his music as a tribute to his Lord. Even at twenty-five, the composer showed true humility for having realized his goal of providing musical vehicles for the furthering of his faith. In the process of following his calling, Handel had also become the most acclaimed composer in Europe.

The top musicians in England sent Handel an invitation to join them, and the composer answered. The composer loved the modern city of London, believed English theater to be the world's best, and felt inspired by the progressive thinking he found in the nation. Yet more than just the environment of what was then the world's greatest city, Handel loved the English language. He felt his prose worked best in the tongue of King James.

In his adopted home, the German-born dynamo reached beyond the oratorios that had made him a star and began to

Hallelujah!
For the Lord God Omnipotent reigneth.
The kingdom of this world
is become the Kingdom of our Lord,
and of His Christ,
and He shall reign forever and ever.
King of Kings, and Lord of Lords,
and He shall reign forever and ever.
Hallelujah!

compose church and secular music, instrumental pieces, operas, and new arrangements of classical works. His work propelled him to the top of his field, and he was made the director of the Royal Academy of Music. Now the most famous musician in England, he had money, power, and respect. Yet his world was hardly perfect. Behind the scenes, a lingering shadow began to haunt the still-young man. It was a demon he could not fight, eventually bringing him to his knees and causing him to question himself, his talents, and his faith.

Even as he ruled the entertainment world, Handel physically began to fall apart. Before he reached forty, he suffered several strokes and was all but crippled by rheumatism. By 1741, his eyesight had failed as well. The world which had once been in such sharp focus was now little more than a blur. Legally blind, barely able to walk, Handel also lost his creative powers. Desperate, the depressed composer spent his savings trying to find cures for his various illnesses. He even paid a surgeon for a crude and painful eye operation. Nothing worked, and with no income from writing, directing, or teaching, Handel went from riches to poverty. Locked in a tiny home on the wrong side of London, he feared his final stop on this earth would be a debtor's prison.

With so many bills due and no way to pay them, the composer dreaded the knock of the mailman. What almost always came were not greetings from old friends but rather duns from bill collectors. But one warm day in August 1742, the mail brought a double dose of good news.

Opening the first envelope, Handel discovered that the Duke of Devonshire wanted the composer to come to Dublin and produce a series of benefit concerts "for the relief of the prisoners in the several goals [jails], and for the support of Mercer's Hospital in Stephen Street, and of the Charitable Infirmary on the Inn's Quay." Anxious to get away from his depressing home, Handel immediately jotted off a note accepting the

Duke's offer. While this first letter seemed like an answered prayer, it would be the second that would change not just Handel's life but the musical world and Christmas itself.

Charles Jennens was a wealthy eccentric whom most folks avoided. Those who knew him labeled his behavior as bizarre. He always seemed to have a new idea to do something a bit differently than anyone had ever done it before, and none of those ideas ever panned out. He seemed to think he had the answer for reorganizing local government, for the redistribution of taxes, or for how children should be properly raised to prevent them from falling into a life of crime. If he heard a sermon, he found ways he would have presented it that were more profound and far-reaching. In fact, he even dared to suggest that Shakespeare's work could be improved. So any letter from Jennens would have been dreaded by most who knew him. Few would have bothered even reading the note, but Handel opened the envelope with a rare zeal for a sick man. His enthusiasm was fueled by the memory of some outstanding poems Jennens had sent him some years before. Maybe, the composer thought, the man had done it again!

Jennens' letter did not contain any original work, but the unique man had developed an idea for a new oratorio. He had started to write it himself but had hit a wall. Remembering Handel's earliest hits, Jennens opted to forward the concept to the composer, hoping it might be a source of inspiration. Little did the man know that the great Handel would not only read his letter but see the potential in its contents.

As he explained in the letter, Jennens had taken what he felt were the most important biblical stories centering on the Messiah and cut them down to what he viewed as the bare-bones essential passages of Scripture. His goal had been to create a new musical presentation from his text, but Jennens simply did not have the talent to start the oratorio, much less complete it. Maybe, he thought, old George would be interested.

Handel was not only interested, for the first time in years he was inspired. On August 22, the composer locked himself in his study and set to work. In seven days he created the first segment of his new musical. This is now known as the "Christmas" section of the *Messiah*. The next part, "The Redemption Story," took nine days. Part three, "The Resurrection and Future Reign of Christ on Heaven and Earth," took another week. After reworking the music several times, Handel felt the new oratorio worthy of a Dublin debut.

On April 13, 1742, with just a handful of singers and a small orchestra, the composer brought the work to life in front of a large audience. Though because of his near blindness he could not clearly see the appreciative crowd, he could tell by its response that he had finally composed another hit. Ultimately the Irish tour was a monumental success for the duke's charities and the composer's career. At home in England, newspapers were declaring that Handel had made a mighty comeback!

A few months later, Handel brought his newest work to the London stage. All of English society was there for the sold-out first few performances. On the second night, King George II was so moved by the first few notes of the "Hallelujah Chorus" that he rose to his feet. When the audience saw the king standing, they followed suit. The composer had no idea what was happening. He could not see the king or anyone else standing. Yet when the "Hallelujah Chorus" ended, and he heard the thunderous applause, he knew he had once again achieved his goal of spreading his faith through his music.

It would be Handel's annual Eastertide performances to benefit his favorite charity, the Foundling Hospital, that would keep him out of debtor's prison and in the public eye for another seventeen years. He conducted his most beloved work a final time just eight days before his death in 1759. Even though he had a library of beloved works to choose from, it was the "Hallelujah Chorus" that played in Westminster Abbey during his funeral. This one element of the *Messiah* was viewed as the great composer's defining moment. Yet with Handel's passing, all of the music from the *Messiah* began to fade away. Soon it was hardly played at all. Even when Wolfgang Amadeus Mozart reworked Handel's old oratorio, no one seemed to care.

A century after Handel's death, the *Messiah* was a piece reserved for local musicals. There were scores of versions, some of them ribald secular settings of the "Hallelujah Chorus," and few were worthy of note. Yet as the Victorian Era reshaped English thinking, the British musical establishment rediscovered Handel's one famed work. Like its writer had done upon the oratorio's creation, by the 1870s the *Messiah* had again emerged from obscurity. It became an Easter favorite of both Protestant and Catholic churches.

By 1900, the *Messiah* was so linked to Easter that people began to expect to hear the oratorio each year. Yet soon a group would move the *Messiah* to Christmas. This was not caused by the sudden realization that the "Hallelujah Chorus" magnified the significance of the celebration of the birth of Christ. Rather it was because Christmas had grown into a holiday that stretched for a month. As people felt more charitable during the holiday season, and as performances of Handel's *Messiah* always sold out during the other important Christian holiday, choir directors decided to stage the oratorio in December as a way to raise money for needed charities. Though he had never intended it to light up the season of the Christ's birth, suddenly the master composer's fabled "Hallelujah Chorus" was the musical centerpiece of the Christmas season.

Charles Burney, the eighteenth-century music historian, remarked that Handel's *Messiah* "fed the hungry, clothed the naked, and fostered the orphan." As a presentation that has raised and continues to raise millions of dollars for charity, it has done all that and more. But it has also accomplished more than being used as a Yule season moneymaker. It has dramatically raised the spiritual awareness of countless millions as well. For millions, the "Hallelujah Chorus" is the most powerful way of remembering the reason for the season.

Webster defines hallelujah as "a shout or song of praise or thanksgiving." Handel would have certainly agreed. He explained to his friends that when he contemplated each act, "I did think I did see all Heaven before me and the great God himself." It would have taken that kind of inspiration to create a work that is so powerful that one song, "Hallelujah Chorus," still brings people to their feet and leads people to the Lord. This wonderful song was more than just a second chance for Handel; it has become perhaps the most powerful musical reminder of the second chance Jesus has given to us all.

2

CHRISTMAS SHOES

On a cold December day in the late 1970s, Helga Schmidt was trying to finish a bit of holiday shopping. As was often the case during Christmas, nothing was easy or quick. Crowds were everywhere, and anxious shoppers were anything but merry as they pushed and shoved to find much-needed gift items. After fighting through grumpy masses to secure a few things from her long list, Schmidt found herself waiting in a seemingly endless, slow-moving checkout line. Just ahead of her in the bustling Kansas store was an obviously excited young boy and girl carefully holding a pair of women's shoes. The gift was so precious to them that they were fighting over who would get to place the box on the counter. After what seemed like an eternity, it finally came time for the kids to pay for the shoes. Anxiously they set them on the counter and watched as the sale was rung up. As the clerk announced the price, the youngsters' hopeful expressions were immediately transformed. Panic gripped them as they looked from the employee, to the shoes, and then to each other.

"Are you sure on the price?" the boy quietly asked.

"Yes," came the flat reply of the exhausted clerk.

Carefully putting all of their coins and bills on the counter, the disappointed pair looked back at the clerk. She quickly fingered through the small stack of silver and copper before coldly announcing, "You're three dollars short."

"Are you sure?" the girl pleaded. "This is all the money we have."

"Then you'll have to put the shoes back and buy something else," the clerk snapped. "Now move along; you're holding up the line."

Even though she was in a hurry to get home, suddenly Schmidt found the small drama unfolding in front of her much more important than her pressing engagements. As she watched the children start to pick up their coins, she sensed that this pair of shoes was extremely important to the brother and sister. She could tell by the way they had held the box, and by the way they pleaded with the store employee, that this gift was more than an afterthought. It had a much deeper meaning.

Digging into her purse, Helga yanked out her pocketbook. Reaching inside, she retrieved three crisp dollar bills. Leaning down toward the siblings, she quietly offered, "Here are the three dollars you need."

The boy and girl didn't hesitate, hastily grabbing the money with an energy indicating both great relief and deep desperation.

"Thank you," they simultaneously whispered. "Thank you so much!"

Handing the money to the clerk, two sets of exhilarated eyes watched as the woman punched the cash register's keys, slipped the money in the drawer, and placed the shoes into a paper bag. Once they had finally been handed their purchase, the boy and girl turned to Helga and thanked her once again.

"You are very welcome," the woman answered. She then observed, "This gift must mean a lot to you."

"The shoes are for our mother," the little girl explained. "She's very sick and is going to heaven real soon."

"These shoes," the boy cut in, "will match the streets of gold in heaven. We learned about those streets in Sunday school class." Clutching their package as if it was the most precious prize on earth, the duo then walked toward the exit.

Helga, now misty-eyed and still stunned by their explanation, watched them for a second before the clerk's "Will this be all?" snapped her back to reality. Nodding, the woman again turned her attention to the two happy children as they pushed open the store's heavy glass door and disappeared into the night.

Later, as she drove home, Schmidt realized that the faith displayed by those children had been worth much more than the three dollars she had given them. Those youngsters had put Helga's focus on the real reason Christ came to earth. Christmas was suddenly not just about a babe in the manger; it was a time to celebrate what the Lord's whole life and ultimate sacrifice really meant to each person in the whole world. And my, she thought, how those children understood the real power of that message!

At the time, Schmidt was taking a continuing education course. Though she hadn't planned on sharing what she had seen at the store, for a class assignment she decided to write about her experience. Not only did Helga earn high marks for her work but her instructor submitted the paper to a local church for their newsletter. First printed in that small publication, the story of the Christmas shoes began to be passed along to other church periodicals. It finally ended up in the bestselling book *Chicken Soup for the Christian Soul*. By the time this book took the touching tale to the world, Schmidt's name had been forgotten.

Lost among all of the other classic anecdotes in the Chicken Soup series, the story of the Christmas shoes might have been completely disregarded if not for the internet. In the late 1990s, this tale of two children giving everything they had to purchase their mother a pair of special shoes for heaven became one of the most popular emails forwarded on the very busy worldwide web. Millions read it. In a way, Helga's experience would become one of the information age's first electronic Christmas cards. But for this story to really take flight, it had to be transformed into another artistic format.

Newsong, a Dove Award–winning group made up of Matt Butler, Eddie Carswell, Billy Goodwin, Michael O'Brien, and Scotty Wilbanks, really took off in the mid-1990s. It was at that time that the quintet initiated a streak of seventeen number-one singles on Christian radio playlists. But what surprised much of the media was that this Christian group, singing songs of a faith-filled lifestyle, also generated airtime on mainstream pop radio stations. Their "Arise, My Love," "Red Letter Day," and "People Get Ready" became crossover hits that made them favorites of hundreds of thousands of young Americans. Thanks to the internet, their fans could keep track of their every move, as well as come to know the faith behind their music. These web-savvy fans could also forward the guys their favorite stories.

During the months leading up to the final Christmas of the twentieth century, while looking through his email, Newsong's Eddie Carswell discovered the heavily forwarded story of the Christmas shoes. After reading it several times, Carswell decided that it needed to be redone in a musical format. He approached a former member of the band to help him compose the number.

"We read this story, and we knew something was there," Carswell explained, "so we kept stabbing at it, kept coming back to it."

Finally Carswell and Leonard Ahlstrom put together a haunting melody line and coupled it with lyrics that remained true to what Helga Schmidt had witnessed two decades before in a Kansas store. All of the group's members were excited by the new holiday song, and Newsong recorded and released the number in time for the twenty-first century's first Christmas season. The group hoped their carol would generate at least a bit of play on mainstream radio. But since many stations were cutting back their holiday music offerings, the space for fresh material was limited. In the final month of 2000, most of what programmers placed on playlists were the traditional carols that had been part of the musical landscape for generations. So it seemed "The Christmas Shoes" was a present that would soon be lost in the blinding and crowded swirl of the season's sounds and events.

Beginning in early December in the Midwest, a few stations finally put "The Christmas Shoes" on limited rotation. Those stations expected little from the Newsong release, so they were not prepared for the response they received. Immediately after the carol's initial play, request lines lit up asking to hear the carol again. The pattern repeated itself at every station that played the new release. "Everyone was calling in to their radio stations," Eddie Carswell explained.

One St. Louis disc jockey reported that for six hours after "The Christmas Shoes" first hit their airwaves, the station's phone lines were completely tied up. Callers were trying to get through to share stories of how their mothers had sacrificed for the holidays and what that sacrifice had meant to them. Others wanted to know what had happened to the brother and sister in the story and how they could help them.

Listeners who heard "The Christmas Shoes" in the limited markets where it found airplay began to email their friends, extolling the song's powerful message of giving and salvation. This one-on-one sharing created a nationwide outpouring of people calling other radio stations demanding to hear Newsong's Christmas carol. Simply due to its powerful message, within three weeks the internet-inspired single hit number one on *Billboard*'s Adult Contemporary chart. It also topped Christian charts and was added to R&B and country playlists.

Because no one had expected much from the new carol, the music industry began to call it "the little song that could." It should have been dubbed "the little song that could not be stopped."

Nashville-based author Donna VanLiere heard Newsong's carol and penned a fictional novel based on the story. Published by St. Martin's Press, the book hit the *New York Times* bestsellers' list.

Sensing the story's potential, the Columbia Broadcasting Company ordered a screenplay based on both the book and the song. In 2002, Rob Lowe and Kimberly Williams starred in the CBS movie that immediately became a holiday classic.

As "The Christmas Shoes" emerged as the first major Christmas hit of the new century, back in Kansas, Helga Schmidt watched, smiled, and thought back to the moment that inspired the story. What if she had been so busy with her holiday shopping that she had not taken the time to look and listen to the children in front of her that day? What if she had allowed them to return the shoes to the store shelves and had not given them the three dollars to complete the purchase? What if those two had never been able to give their mother that final Christmas gift?

"The Christmas Shoes" is a product of the information age. The song was written solely because of an email that had been forwarded tens of thousands of times. But the inspiration for "The Christmas Shoes" is as old as the Christmas story itself. It is about the bond between humanity and God and about belief in a child's faith and actions. Therefore this Christmas carol, while focusing on events in a modern age, is really showcasing the birth of Christ in a manger and the words found in John 3:16. Thus the first popular carol to be launched in the twenty-first century may become one of the most remembered of all time.

3

LET THERE BE PEACE ON EARTH

*I*n the past two thousand years there have been very few Christmas days in which the entire world was at peace. Battles of some kind have been raging on either a regional or global scale since the time when Christ brought his message of peace and goodwill to the earth. Thus while the war to end all wars seems always to be so tantalizingly close, the reality of this dream also appears impossible to ever fully realize.

On a personal level, many individuals who live in peaceful surroundings seem to rarely find peace in their own lives. They fight daily battles with demons that no one else can see, constantly waging war with their insecurities. Each day millions drift closer to the thin line that separates life from death, more often seeing the dark cloud of hopelessness rather than the sunlight brought through faith.

In the days just before the conclusion of World War II, Jill Jackson was just such a despondent woman. She was fighting a life-and-death war with herself. As she studied the enemy, the odds seemed against her. Jill's husband had left her and she had no means of supporting her daughter; she was adrift and lost with few career options. Unable to see beyond the problems that consumed her each waking moment, with her faith shattered, on a very dark night Jill gave up on ever finding any peace on earth.

27

"My mother was brought up in a very rough way," her daughter, Jan Tache, recalled. "My grandmother died when Mom was just three. When my grandfather remarried, my mom's new stepmother was not at all interested in Mom. My grandfather and his wife gave Mom up and she became a ward of the court."

As an unwanted child, Jill suffered terribly. Even before she experienced her first day of school, she was completely alone, with no one telling her she had any value whatsoever. She constantly prayed for a loving family, but with each new rejection she came to believe she did not have enough value to appeal to anyone. When she finally graduated from high school and moved out of state-sponsored care, she was completely unsure of herself. Perhaps in an effort to hide behind different masks or to find self-worth in someone else's life, Jill became an actress.

"She starred in some western movies," Jan explained, "then she married my father, who was a director. For a while they had a wonderful life."

When her daughter was born, Jill felt as if she were living a fairy tale. She had an incredible home, was a part of a social circle that included many of the biggest stars in Hollywood, and seemed to be wanted and loved by everyone. Yet she would soon discover that her happiness was little more than a fleeting illusion. With little warning, Jill's husband grew tired of monogamy and left the young bride and his daughter. As she watched the man she loved drive away, Jill fell into a well of deep despair. The horrors of her childhood again haunted her. She constantly reminded herself she had been deserted by a mother who died, a stepmother who didn't want her, and a husband who found others much more appealing. Ultimately it was simply more than she could take.

"Unable to cope with all the disappointments in her life, Mother tried to commit suicide," Jan recalled. "But she only managed to partially paralyze herself."

Let there be peace on earth, and let it begin with me;
let there be peace on earth, the peace that was meant to be.
With God as our Father, brothers all are we.
Let me walk with my brother in perfect harmony.
Let peace begin with me; let this be the moment now.
With every step I take, let this be my solemn vow;
to take each moment and live each moment in peace eternally.
Let there be peace on earth, and let it begin with me.

As Jill slowly recovered from her suicide attempt, she began to search for peace in life rather than comfort in death. In her search, Jill began sifting through the differing practices of all the world's religious faiths. After exploring all over the globe and throughout the pages of recorded history, she finally found real security through the words of Jesus Christ. With a newly refreshed Christian perspective, Jill escaped the dark times for good.

At the end of World War II, not only was America again at peace, but Jill felt totally at peace herself. It was then, after she had come to know God in a real way, that she met Seymour "Sy" Miller. The Brooklyn-born Miller was an arranger and producer for Warner Brothers. Though now best remembered for writing TV theme songs and preparing nightclub acts for Debbie Reynolds, Andy Williams, Danny Kaye, and Joel Gray, Sy was an all-around musical genius. Yet what appealed to Jill was not his talents but Sy's gentle and caring nature.

"Sy was the most ethical person my mother had ever met," Jan explained. "She loved him dearly, and he loved everything about her, including me. When they got married, it was not only a wonderful thing for her life, but for mine as well."

While Sy worked with movie and recording stars, Jill dabbled in creating her own music. Coming from a background where children had little value, the new Mrs. Miller plunged into writing songs for kids. She called them her "safety net" tunes. These were easy-to-sing and easy-to-remember life-lesson numbers that quickly found homes in school music books and on Little Golden Records.

As Sy and Jill settled into their happy union, the forties became the fifties and another war broke out, this one in Korea. Though now at peace with herself, Jill found it disconcerting to see a new generation of children becoming orphans. She soon realized that in the age of the atom bomb, the world was as bent on destroying itself as she had been when she had tried to take her life. Jill urgently wanted to do something that would make the world take a long look at the consequences of war. In 1955, to answer this call, the wife, mother, and songwriter turned to music.

As Jill outlined her goal for a new song, she told her husband they had a duty not just to wish for peace but also to write something that would inspire individual people to bring this dream to reality. When she read that a group of teenagers from all over the world would soon be attending a "brotherhood" camp not far from their California home, she found a message that would become her best-loved composition and a reflection of her soul. The words came easily, tumbling out of her heart like water over a cliff. When she completed her lyrical message, Jill turned the project over to her husband. It was Sy who developed the melody for "Let There Be Peace on Earth."

To complete what she believed was her call, Jill took the song to the camp organizers. When the directors heard this optimistic anthem, they invited the husband-and-wife team to teach it to the high school kids attending the camp. A few weeks later, on a beautiful summer evening, a group of 180 teenagers of all races and religions formed a circle and sang this new song of peace for the very first time. The song made a huge impact on the kids at the camp, and a few news stories were issued proclaiming the power of the mountaintop debut of "Let There Be Peace on Earth." But sadly, the song did not immediately catch on. It would not be until Americans were fighting in Vietnam that Jill's musical prayer began to be noticed around the globe.

"My parents tried to give the song away," Jan recalled. "They published it but refused to sell it. They just wanted school and church choirs to use it for free. Yet they soon discovered people didn't feel there was any value in something that was simply given away. It was only when they started selling the music that people began to take note."

By 1960, "Let There Be Peace on Earth" was being used in school graduations, PTA programs, and church choirs. It was also adopted as the theme for Veteran's Day, Human Rights Day, and United Nations Day. Groups as varied as the United Auto Workers, the American Legion, B'nai B'rith, the Kiwanis Clubs, and CORE began to sing it at their meetings. Five years later, the song had been translated into scores of languages and become popular in Holland, England, Italy, France, Germany, Lebanon, Japan, India, and several nations in Latin America.

Though "Let There Be Peace on Earth" never hit *Billboard* magazine's top forty, Ernie Ford, Andy Williams, Danny Kaye, Nat King Cole, the Smothers Brothers, Roy Rogers, Dale Evans, Eddie Albert, Edie Adams, Gladys Knight, Mahalia Jackson, Bob Hope, and more than a hundred other artists recorded it. As more and more people heard it, the song was awarded scores of honors including the Brotherhood Award from the National Conference of Christians and Jews.

Most felt that Sy and Jill's anthem would fade away after the end of the Vietnam War. Yet just as Jill Jackson had once searched for peace and discovered it in the words and life of Christ, Christians began to relate her song to the Christmas season. As Christ was known as the Prince of Peace, this seemed a natural union of holiday and music. In fact, what better way to remember Jesus' birth than to sing a song that places the responsibility for bringing peace on earth on the shoulders of his people?

A thrice-rejected woman, haunted by her insecurities, once looked for peace in a place that almost ended her life. Yet as Jill Jackson climbed out of the dark hole in which she had been cast, she discovered that peace had always been there waiting for her through God's Son. Armed with faith, she became a voice for world peace, courageously taking the message of man's brotherhood around the globe. Jill Jackson is now dead and her dream of world peace has not yet been realized, but "Let There Be Peace on Earth" remains as a reminder that Christ's purpose should be embraced not just on December 25th but every day of the year.

SANTA CLAUS IS
COMING TO TOWN

here once was a time when Christian artists would not
think of recording a secular holiday standard. Yet led
by the likes of Point of Grace and Amy Grant, contemporary gospel singers have warmed up to songs that not only
proclaim the birth of the Savior but also tell the story of the
holiday's most beloved fictional character. Why have so many
Christian artists now embraced standards such as "Rudolf the
Red-Nosed Reindeer" and "Here Comes Santa Claus"? Probably because these whimsical numbers don't just spotlight the
childlike wonders of a modern secular Christmas, but they also
offer a bit more. Hidden beneath carefree lyrics are secular
parables spotlighting the rewards of compassion, and understanding and living life within the bounds of moral rules. Of all
these numbers, "Santa Claus Is Coming to Town" is perhaps
the most "out front" with its morality play.

Many families try to run from Santa, feeling that his presence obscures the Christian elements of the holiday. Yet it
hasn't always been that way. In fact, St. Nick was once looked
on as an example of the way a Christian should respond to
children in need. The jolly old elf, as we know him now, was
directly linked to the church.

Over fifteen hundred years before Americans embraced Santa Claus, Eastern European and Western Asian children anxiously awaited the annual visits of St. Nicholas. Nicholas was once a real person. So his legend, as well as the roots of Santa Claus, are based on the story of a good and caring Christian man.

Nicholas was born into a wealthy family just three centuries after the birth of Jesus. At seventeen he gave up his wealth and surrendered to serve the Lord as a monk and missionary. While still in his twenties, he was elevated to the position of archbishop of Myra, an area now in Turkey. Throughout his ministry, Nicholas sought out those the Bible called "the least of these." The red-coated bishop felt it was his mission to reach the downtrodden, the hungry, the sick, and the oppressed. Going against the traditions of the day, Nicholas did not limit his ministry to adults. In a world that largely ignored kids, he taught children, as well as giving them special gifts. Hence, his visits were eagerly anticipated by young and old alike.

When Nicholas died around the year 340, others picked up where the future saint had left off. Church officials, parents, and even local community leaders secretly continued to give gifts on December 6, the anniversary of Nicholas's death. Over the centuries the tradition endured, but with something new added. St. Nicholas no longer gave gifts to all children; he gave them only to those who had been good. Thus children who were obedient to their parents and the teachings of Jesus received a much-desired treasure in their shoes, such as candy or a coin. Those who had not been on their best behavior received only a lump of coal. Many centuries passed, but even as the day for delivering gifts moved to Christmas Eve and Nicholas established his home at the North Pole and changed his name to Santa, the good and bad clause remained locked into a child's holiday contract.

As a very poor boy growing up in rural Kentucky during the final decade of the 1800s, Haven Gillespie's mother often reminded each of her children that Santa not only knew when they were sleeping, but like the good Lord, he also knew when they were good or bad. Fearing the consequences, the clan took their mother's words to heart and tried to live moral lives. Though none of the ten Gillespie children were perfect, it seemed their conduct was always up to the standards to be fondly remembered on Christmas Eve.

Haven left high school at sixteen and found a job as a type-setter at the *Cincinnati Times Star*. A few years later he moved east and began a career writing copy for the *New York Times*. In his spare time he penned Tin Pan Alley tunes for vaudeville acts. In 1911, at the age of twenty-three, Haven signed with Leo Feist, Inc., a music publisher, and launched a career that would land him in the Songwriter's Hall of Fame. Though his most remembered contribution to America's music library would embrace the holidays, for the first two decades of his stellar career Gillespie wrote songs meant for the era's hottest performers.

In the early 1930s, New York song stylist, humorist, and radio star Eddie Cantor began to look for a children's Christmas song. As summer turned to fall and no number turned up, a desperate Cantor began to make calls to various New York music publishers. One of those he contacted was Leo Feist. Feist assured the radio star that he had just what the doctor ordered and he would deliver it to Cantor within a week. In truth Feist had nothing, but he took a large leap of faith because he was confident Haven Gillespie could deliver a song Cantor would love.

Haven was not in a jubilant mood when he entered Feist's office on that same nippy fall day. One of his brothers had just died and Gillespie was in shock. Naturally the only words tumbling over in his creative mind were laced with sadness and regret. So he balked at writing a happy Christmas number. He pointed out that even on good days he only wrote musicals, love songs, and novelty numbers, not kids' tunes.

"This could be big for us," Feist pleaded, before adding that Gillespie was the only songwriter at the firm who had the right vocabulary for children's songs. The publisher pushed, begged, and even demanded that the songwriter at least try to create something for Cantor. Yet he could simply not get through to Gillespie.

An unconvinced Haven left his publisher's office, his mind overflowing with grief. As he boarded the subway to journey back to his apartment, Gillespie began to recall special times with his family. Ironically, it seemed the best memories were of Christmas in the Kentucky hills of his youth. Removing an envelope from his coat pocket, Haven began to jot down what he recalled of those long past holidays. The one picture that continually came to him was his mother's warnings about behaving. He could still clearly hear her saying, "You better watch out, you better be good, because Santa Claus is soon coming to town."

On the back of that used envelope, Gillespie hurriedly jotted down the way his mother had framed both Santa and his mission. As if spurred on by forces he could not fathom, a poem poured from his heart and landed on the paper. Before he had even traveled across the city to his residence, Gillespie finished the unforgettable lyrics to "Santa Claus Is Coming to Town."

Unlike Haven, John Coots was a New Yorker from birth. His mother taught him to play the piano, and in doing so, forever changed the young man's life. In 1914, fresh out of high school, Coots began working for a Wall Street bank. Yet even though the money was good, office hours and adding numbers bored him. So after just three years he gave up financial security and a job with a future to pitch his self-penned tunes. He probably met Gillespie in the early twenties when both of them were writing material for Sophie Tucker. Yet it would not be until 1934 when the duo would come together to create one of Christmas's greatest hits.

Coots, whose works had already lit the Great White Way and found their way to the silver screen, was asked to put music to the lyrics Gillespie had written on the New York subway. He was told this had to be a rushed job. As he studied the poem, he discovered the words had a clickity-clack feel like wheels going over rails. The musician latched onto this rhythmic feel and quickly scored a melody. When he finished, he sent the music back to Leo Feist, and the publisher delivered the new number to Eddie Cantor.

Cantor immediately loved the musical feel and the child-like qualities of the song. He introduced it to the world during his 1934 Thanksgiving network radio show and then sang it again and again as he rode in the annual Macy's Parade. With the record already pressed and on its way to stores, Eddie was ready for a big hit. He was not to be disappointed. "Santa Claus Is Coming to Town" sold more than thirty thousand copies in its first week of release.

Coots, whose hall of fame career would see his songs recorded by the likes of Sinatra, Martin, Page, and Presley, would revel in the success of "Santa Claus." This little children's song was the composer's pride and joy. Before his death in 1985, the Christmas classic would sell more than sixty million copies and be recorded by hundreds of different artists. It stands today as not only one of the most popular Christmas songs of all time but one of history's most beloved children's classics.

For Gillespie the emotions stirred up each holiday season by "Santa Claus" had the opposite effect. Haven always associated the song with his brother's death. So while it conjured up the whimsical nature of Christmas for millions, for the man who composed the lyrics, it rarely brought much joy.

For most this little ditty is nothing more than a fleeting glance at a fictional elf. Yet the story behind Santa and the story behind the song confirm that it is so much more. A dynamic missionary was the template for Santa Claus. Today, thanks to the legend that sprang from his Christian work, the giving spirit of Nicholas illuminates each holiday season. The song that embraces the annual visit of Santa also profiles a poor Kentucky woman's efforts to impress on her children the rewards of living a life of obedience. Thus, "Santa Claus Is Coming to Town" is about much more than just a fat man bearing gifts; it is a musical tribute embracing the timeless values of being the best you can be, a parable not just for the time it was written but for all time.

5

O CHRISTMAS TREE

*I*f England's Queen Victoria had not married Prince Albert of Germany in 1840, the Christmas tree might still be a tradition limited to only Eastern and Central Europe. Yet because Albert brought the holiday traditions of his native country with him when he moved to Buckingham Palace, the fir tree grew into a worldwide symbol of the holiday season. The use of the tree spread so quickly that by 1845 Christmas trees were not only popular in most English households but were spreading like wildfire in Canada and America as well. Yet while it was a prince who jump-started this beloved tradition, it was anything but an overnight success. In fact the custom of the Christmas tree began hundreds of years before the English or Germans crowned their first king. The tree's origins can be traced to the dark and cold Scandinavian winters. In the case of this famous carol, without the Vikings, the song "O Tannenbaum" would never have been written and Albert would never have decorated a fir tree.

A thousand years ago, long before they were first reached by Christian missionaries, superstitious Vikings found hope and strength in the evergreen tree. The evergreen not only lived, but seemed to thrive when times were the most bleak. In an effort to bring some of the tree's magic into their own lives, these warriors would chop down a fir and place it in their homes. They hoped that the spirit of the tree that never

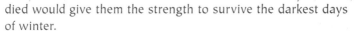

died would give them the strength to survive the darkest days of winter.

Over time others throughout Europe latched onto the Viking custom. In almost all cases they were looking for magic and thought the fir tree to be filled with the power of life. Even the new converts of Christ fell under the spell of the evergreen, but in their case it was not the tree that provided the power but the God who created that tree.

In the dark ages Christians would cut down fir trees, string them with fruit, and use them in religious plays. These paradise trees represented the tree of knowledge in the garden of Eden. Through these pageants, children were taught about the majesty of a loving God. For centuries these plays flourished, but by the late 1500s the practice of displaying the paradise tree had been largely forgotten. Yet in Germany, even though the tradition of religious plays had disappeared, fir trees were still chopped down and brought inside each winter. Except now the meaning was not associated with the first story of the Old Testament but had changed its focus to the first pages of the New Testament.

In the midst of hard German winters, the evergreen took on a representation of Christ's undying love for his people. That love was represented by the fact the tree was as vibrant and alive in the midst of the year's darkest days as it was in the summer's bright light. Using the tree as a symbol, Martin Luther explained the everlasting nature of God's love. It was Luther who probably first pointed out that the evergreen's color did not fade, just as the Lord's love would not fade no matter the circumstance or trial. And the candles he placed on the tree represented the light and hope that Christ brought to the world with his birth and his resurrection. Thus, to those who knew Luther, the tree evolved into a symbol not just of the first Christmas but of all elements of Christian faith.

Thanks in large part to Luther's influence, the Christmas tree became one of the most important holiday symbols of Germany and Austria. So it seems natural that the roots of "O Christmas Tree" can be traced to Luther's homeland.

The origin of the carol's tune is sketchy, but some musicologists believe the song was probably written in medieval times. Though parts of the melody might have been composed in the days of knights, ladies, and crusades, it is unlikely any of the lyrics were penned then. After all, why would someone have been inspired to write a song about a Christmas tree when the only Christian use of the evergreen was in traveling pageants? So Luther's vision of the tree would actually have to wait several centuries before being fully explained in song and coupled with the old folk melody.

The tune we now associate with "O Christmas Tree" was first published in 1799 in the German songbook *Melodien zum Mildheimischen Liederbuch*. Though no authorship was then given to the work, it was most likely based on a Westphalian folk song. When published it was entitled "Es Lebe Hock" and had no connection to the holiday season.

Some twenty years later, August Zarnack published a version of "Es Lebe Hock" with new lyrics. Zarnack was a well-known collector of folk songs, so the words he assigned to the old tune might well have come from his research. Yet while the melody was borrowed, it is now believed by most historians that the forty-four-year-old teacher actually penned at least the first verse and possibly the second. Whether the words were original or taken from another source, there can be no doubt that Zarnack's work was inspired by the ancient folk song "O Dannebom (O Fir Tree)."

> O Dannebom, O Dannebom,
> du drägst "ne grönen Twig,
> den Winter, den Sommer,
> dat doert de leve Tid.

O Christmas tree, O Christmas tree,
Thy leaves are green forever.
O Christmas tree, O Christmas tree,
Thy beauty leaves thee never.
Thy leaves are green in summer's prime,
Thy leaves are green at Christmas time.
O Christmas tree, O Christmas tree,
Thy leaves are green forever.

O Christmas tree, O Christmas tree,
Much pleasure doth thou bring me!
O Christmas tree, O Christmas tree,
Much pleasure doth thou bring me!
For every year the Christmas tree,
Brings to us all both joy and glee.
O Christmas tree, O Christmas tree,
Much pleasure doth thou bring me!

O Christmas tree, O Christmas tree,
Thy candles shine out brightly!
O Christmas tree, O Christmas tree,
Thy candles shine out brightly!

Each bough doth hold its tiny light,
That makes each toy to sparkle bright.
O Christmas tree, O Christmas tree,
Thy candles shine out brightly!

O Christmas tree, O Christmas tree!
Thou tree most fair and lovely!
O Christmas tree, O Christmas tree!
Thou tree most fair and lovely!
Thou dost proclaim the Savior's birth,
Good will to men and peace on earth.
O Christmas tree, O Christmas tree!
Thou tree most fair and lovely.

O Christmas tree, O Christmas tree!
Thou has a wondrous message!
O Christmas tree, O Christmas tree!
Thou has a wondrous message!
Thou dost proclaim the Savior's birth,
Good will to men and peace on earth.
O Christmas tree, O Christmas tree!
Thou has a wondrous message.

O Christmas tree, O Christmas tree,
O evergreen unchanging.
A symbol of good will and love,
You'll ever be unchanging.
Each shining light, each silver bell,
No other sight spreads cheer so well.
O Christmas tree, O Christmas tree,
You'll ever be unchanging.

O Christmas tree, O Christmas tree!
How are thy leaves so verdant?
O Christmas tree, O Christmas tree,
How are thy leaves so verdant?
Not only in the summertime,
But even in winter is thy prime.
O Christmas tree, O Christmas tree,
How are thy leaves so verdant?

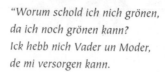

"Worum schold ich nich grönen,
da ich noch grönen kann?
Ick hebb nich Vader un Moder,
de mi versorgen kann.

"Un de mi kann versorgen,
dat is de leve Gott,
de leet mi wassen und grönen,
drum bin ich stark un grot."

The original verses essentially reflect the unchanging nature of the evergreen tree. It is the same always, and as he set to work updating this old song, this fact caused Zarnack to consider the everlasting and unchanging nature of God's love.

Zarnack seemed to aim his new version of the old song at kids. In retrospect, it seemed the teacher-composer's goal was to imprint on children Luther's Christian vision of the tree. Thus the songwriter who put the holiday words to the old folk tune might well have been one of the first Christians to make sure "the reason for the season" was not lost in the more secular celebrations of the day.

Four years later, in 1824, Ernst Anschuetz, another German composer and teacher, added two more verses to Zarnack's Christmas carol. A student of theology, Anschuetz built on what Zarnack had published, again emphasizing the Christian themes Luther had assigned to the tree. It is now thought the composer employed this method of writing to further move the tree away from pagan rituals and cement the association with only Christian Christmas celebrations.

Whatever the inspiration of the two men, the marriage of Zarnack's and Anschuetz's work, coupled with the old folk tune, worked. By 1830 "O Tannenbaum" had become so popular throughout Germany that almost every schoolchild could sing it from beginning to end. Yet it would not find a place outside of this region until England embraced the tradition of the Christmas tree.

Prince Albert might have been the first person in Britain to sing "O Tannenbaum," but others soon jumped on the holiday bandwagon. Translated into English, with new verses added by unknown authors, "O Christmas Tree" spread as quickly as the custom of placing fir trees in parlors during the Christmas season. Within a decade, it even became an English tradition to sing "O Christmas Tree" upon completion of the Christmas Eve tree decorating.

Introduced in the United States in the mid-1840s, the song quickly found favor. There can be no doubt that the rapid assimilation into American culture was due in part to the fact that everyone already knew the tune. It had been coupled with scores of other lyrics popular with settlers going back to Jamestown and Plymouth Rock. Yet even though its use as one of the most popular holiday songs easily eclipsed everything that had come before, it did not mean that "O Christmas Tree" would be the only future American song to embrace the old folk tune. Today Maryland, Michigan, and Iowa all employ this ancient melody for their state song. Yet while those living in those three states might think of their states when they hear the strains of the familiar melody, for most around the globe the images this tune conjures up reflect Christmas and evergreens.

With the advent of the recording industry, "O Christmas Tree" was one of the first holiday songs to find its way into the studio. Over the decades, Nat King Cole, Bing Crosby, and a parade of other artists have placed their mark on this old German offering and made it one of the most recorded seasonal favorites. Yet, as it began its life as a children's song, it seems appropriate that today it is mainly children who keep this old classic alive. And what a wonderful song for kids to sing. Not only does "O Christmas Tree" provide a musical history of the use of the fir tree during the holiday season, but its lyrics also embrace the never-ending presence of God, the eternal nature of faith, and the promise of everlasting life that can be found not just on December 25 but every day of the year. In a very childlike way, "O Christmas Tree" is a musical Sunday school lesson using the wonder of a decorated fir tree to tell the story of God's never-ending love for his people.

THANK GOD FOR KIDS

One of the great traditions of any Christmas season is the continued performances of Handel's *Messiah*. For more than a century and a half, this great musical has been used to raise funds for some of the world's greatest charities. In the last two decades, a new song has become a second key holiday tradition employed in obtaining donations to children's charities. Like the *Messiah*, this moving musical tribute was not intended to become a Christmas carol, and yet thanks to its timeless message, "Thank God for Kids" has emerged as one of the season's most touching and meaningful carols and an effective fundraising tool.

One of America's most honored vocal quartets, the Oak Ridge Boys, was the first to cut "Thank God for Kids." In 1982, when the group loaned their voices to Eddy Raven's newly written autobiographical number, few believed it would be a hit. While it was a wonderful song with a deeply moving message, it did not fit the profile needed to gain radio play on country or pop music stations. The song's story of how much children mean to a father did not seem to carry much chart power. Yet somehow "Thank God for Kids" defied the odds, racing up *Billboard*'s playlist and peaking at number three during the 1982 holiday season. Though it was not meant to be a Christmas song, music fans felt it really touched on the most important living element of the holidays ... kids. This unexpected Christmas leap into the nation's

top ten would mark the beginning for a song that has reawak-
ened the giving spirit in millions of people around the globe and
renewed the Bible charge found in Matthew 25:44–45: "They
also will answer, 'Lord, when did we see you hungry or thirsty
or a stranger or needing clothes or sick or in prison, and did not
help you?' He will reply, 'I tell you the truth, whatever you did
not do for one of the least of these, you did not do for me.'"

"I was the oldest of ten," Eddy Raven explained as he
talked about his inspiration for writing "Thank God for Kids."
"So kids have always been a big part of my life. I have two boys
and ten dogs, so I'm always raising something. Anyway, I was
coming back from Lauren, South Carolina, after playing a show
for a friend."

After his concert, another country music entertainer, Johnny
Duncan, got in touch with Eddy. Duncan had been playing a
show very close to Lauren and proposed the two team up for
the ride back to Nashville.

"We stopped at a Smoky Mountain rest stop to eat some
lunch," Raven recalled. "I got to watching these kids sliding
down a mountain. They were having so much fun. I smiled and
said, 'Thank God for kids.'"

The short little prayer for the blessings created by the joy
of children might have been quickly forgotten if Duncan had
not cut in with, "That's a song! You need to write that!"

Though he didn't really have anything but a title, Raven
picked up an old Piggly Wiggly grocery bag and jotted down his
four-word prayer of thanksgiving. When he got home he took
the sack and put it on his "to do" pile. Several weeks later it had
been buried by a host of other song ideas, bills, and notes.

"I remember it was March of 1973," Eddy recalled, "and I
was in my office working on songwriting. I spotted the sack,
looked at the hook, and began to try to put something with it.
I was getting nowhere when my son came in to join me. Ryan

was three or four at the time and carrying his plastic guitar. He asked me what I was doing and after I told him I was writing a song, he asked if he could write one with me."

The singer smiled at the boy and said, "What do you want to write about?"

Ryan thought about his life for a moment, then declared, "Mickey Mouse."

A bit amused but acting very serious, Raven then inquired, "What else?"

"Big Bird." This time the answer came without thinking.

Before he could add anything else, Ryan heard the opening music for *Sesame Street* playing in the next room. Forgetting about composing a new song, he left his father to watch his favorite television program.

Most writers would have laughed at the thought of writing about Mickey Mouse or Big Bird. Not much of a market for either on popular music charts. Yet as Raven considered the two children's icons, he began to think of a few others as well. A thought then struck him. If there were no kids, then there wouldn't be a Mickey Mouse, Big Bird, or even a Santa Claus. There also would not be those many questions that adults always try to answer but never do, like "Daddy, why is the sky blue?" Suddenly, thanks to getting to view the world through his own child's eyes, Eddy now knew how to complete "Thank God for Kids." Scribbling on that brown grocery sack, the writer finished the song in fifteen minutes. As he ran through it the first time, he also realized the lyrics really were a parent's prayer of thanksgiving.

Ron Gent was producing Raven for ABC Records, and when he heard Eddy sing "Thank God for Kids," he was sure it would be a hit. Many had been predicting the artist was about to take the music world by storm; with Ron's backing, Eddy thought this might be his break song. Yet the label felt it was unsuitable for country music audiences. Though he recorded "Thank

God for Kids" and continued to pitch it to his producers, Raven could not convince them of the song's potential. It was finally released as a "B" side in 1975. When that single went nowhere, ABC dropped Eddy. It would be seven years later before the singer found a label that could fully display his talents and take one of his cuts to number one. Sadly, it would take about the same amount of time for Raven's quiet tribute to the wonderful blessings of children to find a home as well.

"I continued to pitch it," Eddy explained, "but everyone in town turned it down. Finally I was playing in Fort Worth, Texas, when someone told me the Oaks were cutting a Christmas album and had two slots left open."

Though it was not a traditional Christmas song, Raven sent it to the group. As they listened to Eddy's original recording, the Oaks fell in love with "Thank God for Kids." They cut it feeling it was vital not only to the album project but to them as well. Just glad that "Thank God for Kids" now was going to be given a chance as a single, the writer didn't find out till much later just how much it meant to the four guys who cut it.

"Duane Allen [the Oaks' lead singer] later told me how important that song was to keeping the band together," Raven recalled. "It struck an important chord for them when they were wondering if they needed to go on."

Before the single hit radio, the Oaks tried it out in front of live audiences. It was a Pine Bluff, Arkansas, crowd that was the first to hear it. Before the group had even finished singing "Thank God for Kids," the audience was standing. The Oaks were amazed as the ovation for this unknown song went on for several minutes. Many who were cheering the loudest were also crying. In the next sixteen concerts, "Kids" drew a standing ovation every night.

For the Oak Ridge Boys, "Thank God for Kids" renewed their energy. Though it did not reach the top of the charts, the group would score eleven number-one recordings in the next five years. So if this single kept them together, then the song was an answer to the quartet's prayers for a reason to stay together and keep singing.

When the holidays came around in 1983, "Thank God for Kids" was picked up by local charities all across the nation. Groups used the song as a way to gain attention for efforts in securing gifts for underprivileged children. Two years later "Kids" was being used nationally by the Shriners to raise money for burn victims. Within a decade of the Oak Ridge Boys' cutting the single, it would be used at Christmas to raise tens of millions of dollars for children by organizations such as Feed the Children and the National Committee for the Prevention of Child Abuse. Recognizing the power of the song, Eddy has even given away his part of the royalties to numerous charity organizations.

"I came up tough," Raven explained. "I would not have made it without a whole lot of folks helping me. I am thrilled something I have done could mean so much for others at Christmas."

"We released this little song," Duane Allen recalled in 2005, "and we thought we just had this cool little song for Christmas. But then the holidays ended and 'Kids' steams on into 1983 and becomes one of our most played songs ever! How cool is that for a major act to have had a huge hit with a song that says, 'Thank God for Kids'?"

Each year "Thank God for Kids" is cut by more and more artists and becomes more strongly linked to the holidays. Though it was never intended to be, it has become a very spiritual Christmas carol.

"I believe that something bigger than me pushes the pen on a song like this," Raven humbly answered when trying to explain the song's incredible appeal. "I was blessed to be holding the pen when the song was written."

One of the best known music authorities in Nashville, Wesley Rose, once told Eddy, "I am not sure if 'Thank God for

Kids' is the best song you have ever written, but I know it is the song that will go on forever."

"Thank God for Kids" has now become one of the most requested holiday songs on radio stations and in concerts. Thanks to its association with Christmas, its mention of the innocent wonder, joy, and curiosity of children, and its heart-felt description of why kids are God's greatest gifts to parents, this singing prayer will no doubt be played for years to come. "Kids" will also continue to awaken a chord in people that constantly reminds them to reach out to the least of these during the most wonderful time of the year.

> When you get down on your knees tonight
> To thank the Lord for his guiding light
> And pray they turn out right
> Thank God for kids.

WE WISH YOU
A MERRY CHRISTMAS

oday, when carolers lend their voices to the strains of "We Wish You a Merry Christmas," it is usually at the conclusion of their performance and only the chorus is sung. No one seems to now ask for figgy pudding or even sing out the good tidings of the season. Though this simple little ditty remains one of the world's best known carols, it is really out of place in a modern world. The Christmas that was celebrated when "We Wish You a Merry Christmas" was a musical holiday centerpiece is now long forgotten, replaced by a holiday that embraces the birth of Christ, a Santa who recalls the wishes of good little children, and a gentle time of families coming together to remember old memories and make new ones. This Christmas of today is far better than the English Christmas of three hundred years ago when figgy pudding was a holiday treat and those singing the song were little more than old-fashioned looters.

"We Wish You a Merry Christmas" was probably written in the sixteenth century. Initially it was performed by "waits," traveling bands of troubadours who sang songs of the season on streets in English cities. These troupes would make their living from the gifts of the wealthy who paid to hear their songs. So initially "We Wish You a Merry Christmas" did evoke pleasant thoughts of a holiday that, ironically, was then often ignored by most Christians in England. Yet when an unsavory group of people took over the song, reshaping its meaning, "We Wish You a Merry Christmas" became an anthem that evoked alarm and consternation.

Though it's not often mentioned today, Christmas was once a lot more like Mardi Gras than a worshipful holiday. This is the reason why Christmas, up until twenty years before the Civil War, was all but ignored in both England and the United States. In Germany and sections of Eastern Europe, the holiday was observed with both awe and reverence, but in the English-speaking world the day had evolved into a time of drunken parties and marauding street gangs, so many upstanding citizens just wanted it to disappear.

Because of pagan elements dating back to the days when Rome ruled the world, for centuries the Protestant church tried to have Christmas abolished. Even after America broke off from Great Britain, celebrating Christmas was a crime in many sections of New England. On December 25, stores and schools in Boston and New York City remained open, Congress met, courts held sessions, and only a few churches unlocked their doors for worship services. Presents were not given out until New Year's, and decorating for the holidays was unheard of.

Though attempts to officially outlaw Christmas in England had failed during the rule of Oliver Cromwell, the holiday did not resemble a "holy" day. In fact, extra police were placed on duty to try to control the drunken crowds who roamed the streets. These revelers had more than simply celebrating on their minds; like pirates sailing the open sea, they were after bounty. Most set their sights on the nicest sections of their communities. As they roamed, they sang songs reflecting their feelings about the day. "We Wish You a Merry Christmas," now sung with a demanding tone, was the most popular of these old carols.

We wish you a Merry Christmas;
We wish you a Merry Christmas;
We wish you a Merry Christmas and a Happy New Year.
Good tidings we bring to you and your kin;
Good tidings for Christmas and a Happy New Year.
Oh, bring us a figgy pudding;
Oh, bring us a figgy pudding;
Oh, bring us a figgy pudding and a cup of good cheer.
We won't go until we get some;
We won't go until we get some;
We won't go until we get some, so bring some out here.
We wish you a Merry Christmas;
We wish you a Merry Christmas;
We wish you a Merry Christmas and a Happy New Year.

During the blackest days of Christmas in old England, though it is now hard to imagine, "We Wish You a Merry Christmas" was not nearly as sweet as the chorus and old English folk tune made it sound. There were many more verses to this old holiday standard than what we know today, and the most important element in understanding the lyrics rests not in the first verse but in the refrains that connect that verse to the chorus.

> *Oh, bring us a figgy pudding;*
> *Oh, bring us a figgy pudding;*
> *Oh, bring us a figgy pudding*
> *and a cup of good cheer.*

> *We won't go until we get some;*
> *We won't go until we get some;*
> *We won't go until we get some,*
> *so bring some out here.*

The key line in the old carol is "We won't go until we get some." This meant exactly what it said. The band of singers would knock on the doors of the finest houses and sing out their demands. If the owners of the homes did not meet the loathsome group's requests, then the men often knocked open the doors and took what they pleased. Thus this form of early caroling became a very serious and sometimes lethal version of "trick or treat." Some homeowners and singers were killed during these visits, and many were injured.

The singing of "We Wish You a Merry Christmas" didn't just announce the arrival of the unwanted band but gave ominous warnings as well. Police and the homeowners usually gauged the seriousness of the situation by carefully listening to the lyrics sung in the song's verses. There were always sighs of relief if only food and drink were mentioned. When the carolers began to demand money or household items, the law and those hearing the song from inside the home became very concerned.

The wild nature of Christmas lasted several hundred years in both England and the United States and did not dramatically change until Santa arrived on the scene. In a very real sense, the figure based on St. Nicholas helped save the holiday for families and churches alike. Santa, along with the great German traditions brought to England by Prince Albert when he married Queen Victoria in 1840, erased the centuries-old image of a violent and lawless Christmas, replacing it with one focusing on the true meaning of the holiday and the spirit of giving. This change in perception was the foundation for the Christmas we know and celebrate today.

With the advent of a gentler holiday, most elements of the ribald Christmas of the past were quickly forgotten. Yet the old street carol "We Wish You a Merry Christmas" lived on. This time it was sung by a new generation of street singers who embraced foremost the holiness of the holidays. These carolers transformed "We Wish You a Merry Christmas" into a number that brought smiles, not fear. Finally it was again a song that was sung with sincere good wishes of a wonderful holiday season.

For the curious who still long to taste figgy pudding, the recipe consists of figs blended with butter, sugar, eggs, milk, rum, apple, lemon and orange peel, nuts, cinnamon, cloves, and ginger. Yet while the ingredients are easy to find today, it would probably not be a popular gift during the modern Christmas season. Like the violent Christmas of the past, figgy pudding might best be forgotten.

8

MERRY CHRISTMAS, DARLING

*O*ne of Christmas's greatest songs of the modern age was inspired by two teenagers sharing a few innocent moments during the summer of 1946. Yet it would take more than two and a half decades for this treasured contemporary carol to be transformed from a sentimental love poem to one of the holiday's most moving ballads.

In the first full summer after the end of World War II, one anxious teenager was counting down the days until the fall term started at St. Olaf College. During this time, the small school, whose roots went back to early Norwegian settlers, was alive with optimism. America and its allies had won the war, freedom had been preserved, and families were again united. Many of the school's former professors and students would be returning to classes for the first time since they left the campus to defend their country. These old friends would be there to welcome new students who were yearning to grow up in a peaceful age. So at St. Olaf, and almost everywhere in the nation, it was a time of hope, and in the midst of this hope bloomed romance.

Frank Pooler was one of the millions who had dreams. Upon getting his degree, he wanted to take part in creating and performing music that reflected the optimism of the times. Yet during the warm summer days, dreams of fame in the entertainment world had taken a back seat to visions of a young woman's beauty.

"Sylvia had come to Northfield from Wisconsin to spend the summer with her sister-in-law," Frank explained. "Sylvia's brother was my former band director. He was still in the service and she had come to visit and help his wife with the kids."

For the young Pooler, June, July, and August were three months of bliss thanks to Sylvia. It was almost as if he was living out an Andy Hardy script. Yet after a summer of movies and long walks, hand-holding, and talking about future dreams, the upcoming school term created an obstacle for the budding romance. So as Sylvia said goodbye and went back east to school, Frank found himself heartsick and alone. For the boy it was as if the sunshine had been replaced by dark clouds and the warm breeze by a cold gale.

In the waning days before the fall semester, Pooler spent a weekend at a quaint little fishing camp. At the sportsmen's resort, he was surrounded by crystal clear streams and lakes, breathtaking tree-covered vistas, and gorgeous blue skies. Yet Frank was too forlorn to notice nature's colorful canvas. Minute by minute he longed only to see his girlfriend's lovely face.

"I was fishing one day out in a lake," Pooler recalled, "and though it was nowhere near Christmas, a lyric came to me. Guess I was thinking about what it would be like to spend a holiday separated from someone you loved."

Frank's love poem, which he called "Merry Christmas, Darling," embraced the same sentiment found in the recent wartime holiday hit "I'll Be Home for Christmas." Yet Pooler's version, while simply written, was longer and more detailed than the Bing Crosby hit. It was a more complex song that took a much deeper look at the loneliness created by separation. After refining his lyrics, the young man composed a melody and completed a musical arrangement. He then made a mental note to create a second copy to send to his summer love. Yet, as often happens with busy college kids, the song was set aside and thoughts of the girlfriend faded away. It would only be after he graduated from St. Olaf that "Merry Christmas Darling" would again be remembered.

"I was working in Boston with a vocal group," Pooler recalled, "and the trio was looking for a Christmas song. I told them I had written one. They heard it, liked it, sang it, and I got 'Merry Christmas, Darling' published."

While Frank now had made inroads into the world of entertainment, few outside of Boston ever heard his holiday love song. As the years passed and Pooler married, moved across the country to California, and became a college instructor, the song was filed away. It probably would have never again been performed if Pooler had not been drawn into a conversation with one of his students at California State at Long Beach.

Richard Carpenter was the pianist for Frank's school choir. The young man had made a great impression on the director. Carpenter was not a typical student. He was both talented and driven. He had an ear for harmonization and an inherent feel for arrangement. Like Frank, Richard also had dreams of making it in entertainment. Even while taking a full course load, Carpenter found the time to put together a small group. His Richard Carpenter Trio performed in local clubs and theaters. The group featured Wes Jacobs and Richard's younger sister Karen on drums and vocals.

"One day as the holidays approached," Pooler explained, "Richard told me he was tired of his group doing standards like 'White Christmas.' He wanted to know if I knew of anything different and new his group could sing. I thought for a moment, then told him I had written a Christmas song a long time ago, but I didn't care much for the tune."

Carpenter then picked up the story. "In 1966, I was enrolled at Cal State Long Beach and was a member of the university choir. Frank Pooler was the director. He had heard some of the little songs I had been composing and Karen had been singing. He liked my melodies. One day he brought me a song he had written in 1946. He told me he didn't like the music but liked the words. I took it to a practice room at lunch to see what I could do with it."

Tucked away by himself in a small cubicle that featured only a piano and a bench, the college student studied his director's original effort. Carpenter thought the lyrics were sound. As is often the case with composers, as Richard read the words, a tune immediately began to take shape in his head. In fact he was so inspired, he was able on his lunch break to compose an entirely new musical framework around Frank's holiday love poem. The next time he saw Pooler, Carpenter presented the instructor with a copy of the new "Merry Christmas, Darling."

"He liked it right off the bat," Richard recalled, "and over the next few years, when we got a few gigs at Christmas parties, we would play the song. But that was about it."

Within a few months of his reworking "Merry Christmas, Darling," Richard and Karen's talent was noted by several West Coast labels. RCA was the first to record them, but it would not be until 1970, when Karen turned twenty, that the A&M label finally offered the Carpenters a real chance at stardom. With Richard in charge of arrangements and Karen's unmistakable voice lighting up each new recording, the group became an overnight sensation. It was the hit "Close to You" that made them superstars with kids and adults.

When "We've Only Just Begun" rocketed up the charts, A&M Records sensed they had a gold mine. To fully capitalize on the Carpenters' success, the label felt they needed a holiday single. The question wasn't whether this was a good idea — it obviously was — but how to do it. Richard and Karen were playing one-night stands all over the country. They rarely got home, much less had time to prepare for a recording session. Yet A&M's Joe Osborne was not going to give up. Noting when the brother-sister team had a few days off, he booked a studio. Convincing the act they needed a holiday record, Osborne then considered what form the project might take. He wondered if Richard and Karen should cut a familiar standard or a new song.

Richard was a perfectionist. The music he created in the 1970s has remained popular and fresh because of the time and effort he put into arranging, producing, and recording each individual cut. He sacrificed nothing, laboring to get even the most seemingly insignificant element of every record perfect. Therefore, to go from not having a plan to creating a finished Christmas release in just a few days was alien to his nature. When he realized that the label had to have a Christmas song, he agreed to do it only if they allowed him to make it a very special musical gift.

To accomplish what both A&M and Richard wanted to achieve, Carpenter turned back to Frank Pooler's lyrics coupled with his own melody. As the group already knew the song and there was a basic arrangement in place, a solid version of "Merry Christmas, Darling" could be cut and mastered in the brief window of time Richard had been given. Still, the pianist-producer worked almost around the clock to make sure nothing was compromised and that the quality of this production would meet or exceed the level of the group's other recordings.

"We put it together in a week," he remembered. "We had three tracks, and we worked on each track first and then put them all together. This was the most cost-effective way to get it done. As it was late in the year, we had to move to get it released."

A&M had been hoping for something quick and adequate to give to a nation craving anything and everything the Carpenters released. Yet what they received from the siblings were a holiday song and a performance that come around only once in a decade. Richard's flowing score, backed by rich layers of harmonies and orchestration, was both simple and breathtaking. Added to this seemingly perfect musical effort were Karen's dynamic vocals. The woman did not as much sing the words as she lived them. She breathed life into Pooler's lyrics. Thanks to this marriage of talent and effort, "Merry Christmas, Darling" was truly a holiday love letter. It was both timeless and timely. It was also a huge holiday hit.

"When I finished producing the song," Richard recalled, "I called Frank Pooler and asked him if he could meet us at Studio B. When he arrived, I played it for him."

"When I got up to the studio and sat down," Pooler added, "Richard punched a button, and this song started playing. I didn't recognize it at first, but then I heard what sounded like my old words."

"I could tell he was blown away." Carpenter added, "I think it is one of the best records we ever made."

"Merry Christmas, Darling" became even more popular a few years later when the Carpenters released their first Christmas album. On this release, along with a wonderful version of their hit single, Richard and Karen performed the well-known and time-tested religious carols they had sung since childhood. With this vibrant collection of spiritual holiday songs and secular favorites, *Christmas Portrait* brought a fresh element to the rock music audience.

"For years after the release of the single," Richard explained, "Karen and I talked about recording a Christmas album. By early 1978 we finally got underway. I wanted the album to play almost as a continuous performance and to feature some lovely lesser-known tunes as well as the standards."

This album, and a second one released after Karen's death, are two of the best-loved and most-popular Christmas offerings of the soft-rock era. As recording projects, they stand apart because of the quality of the recordings. Yet it is the emotional way fans latched on to them that really set these holiday releases apart from hundreds of other seasonal offerings. All the songs struck deep chords with listeners, but even as stations played Carpenter versions of carols such as "O Little Town Of Bethlehem" and "O Holy Night," people continued to request "Merry Christmas, Darling." By the time Karen passed away in 1983, that Carpenters' song had established itself as a vital musical element of each new holiday season. And its popularity continues to grow.

Because of the sincere emotion in Karen's performance and Richard's precise arrangement, "Merry Christmas, Darling" has become an anchor to millions. This carol, inspired by a modest summer romance, is the modern equivalent of "I'll Be Home for Christmas." And almost three decades after it was first released, Richard and Frank still receive boxes of letters and cards from men and women all around the world explaining how much the song means to them.

It took twenty years for a pair of college students from two different generations to come together and create this incredible Christmas classic. Then it was another five years before Pooler and Carpenter's song first found its holiday niche. Over the past thirty years, this love carol has taken on a life of its own as it has evolved into a musical Christmas card that links families together. Though its lyrics contain none of the biblical story of Christmas, the spirit found in the song still wraps the season in a loving embrace that rings true year after year. After all, at the very first Christmas, God gave the purest of all love to all humankind in the gift of a child. Today the Carpenters' "Merry Christmas, Darling" reminds us that pure and unselfish love is still the most important gift to treasure and share during each new holiday season.

Sweet Little Jesus Boy

O ut of the thousands of Negro spirituals written and sung by slaves in the centuries before the Civil War, a scant few survive. Composed by men and women who could neither read nor write, most songs were passed down orally from one generation to the next. Though occasionally appreciated by the whites of the colonial era, these African-American religious folk songs were not published. Often the only way the songs left the plantation where they were written was when a man or woman who knew the number was sold and moved to another location. So while songs like "Swing Low, Sweet Chariot" and "Good Old Gospel Ship" are incredibly moving and powerful musical testimonies of deep suffering and boundless faith, the spirituals which have been forever lost probably offered even greater inspiration and a deeper insight in the lives of the first black Americans. For those who are aware of the music's history, there is usually a hint of sadness that touches the soul whenever a moving spiritual is performed. This hint of depression comes from knowing the chains that bound each of the song's writers and the fact that so many other African-American gospel folk standards have been lost and forgotten.

Spirituals were born from the mixing of African and American folk music. The early slaves brought with them the songs of their homelands. These traditional tribal numbers were much different from the spirituals which now survive. Still, much of

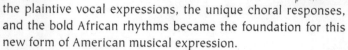

the plaintive vocal expressions, the unique choral responses, and the bold African rhythms became the foundation for this new form of American musical expression.

In the New World, slaves found not only hard work but a new faith. Strange as it might seem, many slave owners considered it their duty to share the gospel with their servants. In scores of plantations, slave churches were created and worship was encouraged. Learning about the figures in the Bible, hearing about the children of Israel and the crucifixion of Jesus, brought hope to those without earthly freedom. The fact that Jesus' death and resurrection had purchased eternal liberty was a subject soon woven into many of the African folk songs.

The first generation of slaves passed down much of their musical heritage to a generation of new slaves born on Southern plantations. Soon these native Americans mixed the sounds of Africa with the music that was a part of the land of their birth. Over time the styles blended into a single harmonious form, choral in nature and driven by emotional lyrics that brought into sharp focus the lives and beliefs of the songs' writers.

It is probably not surprising that most of the surviving spiritual music was created not by house servants but by outdoor laborers. While those doing home chores often found time to visit or even take breaks, the men and women who toiled in the hot sun rarely had time for either. The backbreaking labor usually began before dawn and lasted until the sun went down. The work was not only difficult but tedious as well. Boredom often took an even greater toll than did fatigue. During those long days, entertaining stories, set to music, helped pass the time. As a rule, one singer would sing his song, then another would follow. As the songs became well known, multiple voices would blend together.

Just as is the case with radio requests or song lists on iPods, some of the music became more popular. Thus a few of the numbers were performed much more often. In some

Sweet little Jesus boy,
they made you be born in a manger.
Sweet little Holy Child,
didn't know who you was.
Didn't know you come to save us, Lord;
to take our sins away.
Our eyes was blind, we couldn't see,
we didn't know who you was.
Long time ago, you was born.
Born in a manger low,
Sweet little Jesus boy.
The world treat you mean, Lord;
treat me mean, too.
But that's how things is down here,
we didn't know 'twas you.
You done showed us how, we is trying.
Master, you done showed us how,
even when you's dying.
Just seem like we can't do right,
look how we treated you.
But please, sir, forgive us, Lord,
we didn't know 'twas you.
Sweet little Jesus boy,
born long time ago.
Sweet little Holy Child,
and we didn't know who you was.

cases certain singers also became more popular, and they were asked to lead more often than others. In some cases one voice would take a lead on a spiritual and the remainder of the workers would sing out an answering chorus. Over time, as the compositions became more polished, the voices blended into anthems filling the countryside with breathtaking expressions of heartfelt emotions. Yet sadly, besides the slaves and their owners, there were few in the rural South who ever heard these performances.

The few Negro spirituals which have survived give great insight into what inspired the songs' writers. Many of the best-known spirituals embrace the story of Moses, the flight of Israelites from Egypt to freedom, and the world's rejection of God's own Son. It is no accident that these themes of oppression and freedom run through almost all of the spirituals we know today. After all, the goal of every slave would have been to experience liberty, so the heroes of enslaved people would be those with whom they shared a common bond.

While Christmas was a special holiday through much of the South, it was probably even more precious to the slaves. Christmas was one of the few days of the year these servants did not have to work. A few even received token presents such as new clothing or a special meal from their masters. Because Christmas day was so vastly different from all the others, it was a day greatly anticipated by most African-Americans of the period.

Yet more than a day without work, what really made Christmas so important to slaves was the image of Jesus himself. In the eyes of those in bondage, this boy born in a stable was much more like them than the people who wore the nice clothes and lived in the big houses.

"Sweet Little Jesus Boy" embraces the relationship between slave and Savior better than any of the surviving spirituals. The first few lines quickly establish that Christ was born in a barn and that the world had no clue as to who he was. Certainly a slave could strongly identify with the Lord's humble beginnings.

The song continues by examining Christ through the eyes of a world that knew him not. For a man who was treated as a beast of burden, the thought of being unappreciated was normal. A slave usually sensed his own potential but knew that he would never have a chance to actually realize it. He could dream of earning his freedom with a heroic act that saved his owner's life, but he knew this would likely never happen. Thus he was like Christ in this way as well.

The fact that Jesus was treated harshly by his own people was probably seen more clearly in the writer's eyes than it could have been in the eyes of a free man. And then, when the composer mournfully added, "[They] treat me mean, too. But that's how things is down here," the relationship between Jesus and the slave is fully cemented. They both understand the cold, cruel nature of the sinful world.

This simple spiritual then presents a realization that in both life and death Christ showed the way that everyone should live. And though the slave writer realized neither he nor his master would ever measure up to the Lord's standard of conduct, the composer knew he would be forgiven. Because of Christ's sacrifice and his own belief, in heaven the slave would find himself on equal ground with those who had robbed him of his earthly freedom.

For slaves, simply celebrating the birth of Christ was not enough; they had to know the rest of the story so that they could look to something beyond the bonds of slavery. To them, heaven and the freedom it would bring were the ultimate Christmas gifts. In a scant two verses and a chorus, "Sweet Little Jesus Boy" fulfills this urgent need. The carol tells the story of Jesus being born, living as a model for all people, lay-ing down his life for the salvation of all men, and then rising to join his Father in heaven. First sung in a field by a slave, "Sweet Little Jesus Boy" not only offers an insightful look at the first Christmas but presents the true impact salvation can have on even those in the most hopeless of situations.

SOME CHILDREN SEE HIM

lfred Burt might well be America's greatest composer of Christmas carols. In his brief thirty-three
years, he penned some of the most beloved holiday songs of all time. Each is special, not just because they
so eloquently and beautifully capture the spiritual nature of
the season but also because they were written as gifts. Burt
never intended to sell any of his carols, only share them with
those he loved. Yet thanks in large part to Henry Cole, the
Englishman who in 1843 invented the practice of sending out
Christmas cards, Burt's work would be discovered and his
songs would become an essential element of the holidays for
millions. Burt's beautiful songs continue enriching the season
like few things can.

"It really began with my grandfather," Diane Burt, Alfred's
daughter, explained.

Bates Gilbert Burt was an Episcopal priest who loved everything about the holidays except for the rather generic greeting
cards he sent and received each year. He grudgingly gave the
cards to the postman each December, but with every passing
year he wished he could mail something that more personally
reflected his own joyous views of Christmas. In 1922, Father
Burt was inspired. Rather than buy cards, he opted to pen a
carol, create some original art, and mail musical gifts of the
season to all those he dearly loved. The response he received

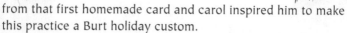

from that first homemade card and carol inspired him to make this practice a Burt holiday custom.

At the Burt household, Christmas was a time of music, decorations, and family gatherings, as well as a time of deeply spiritual prayers and thanksgivings. It was also a time when people invested not just their money in gifts but their talents in giving to others. This could mean caroling, singing at church, or cooking meals for the poor. For the Burts, Christmas was about giving, not just from the pocketbook but also from the heart. It was into this tradition that Albert was born.

"The carols," Anne Burt, Alfred's wife, once wrote, "were as natural an expression of the Burt Christmas as the spicy tree in the rectory or Mother Burt's plum pudding."

Father Burt was a self-taught musician who was somewhat limited by his lack of formal training. The priest was therefore determined his son would have the benefit of all that American education could offer. This was especially true when it came to music. Thus Alfred's music lessons began before his tenth birthday and continued through high school and then college. In 1942, armed with a degree in music from the University of Michigan, the younger Al had grown into an accomplished trumpet player, pianist, vocalist, and composer. At just twenty-two, he seemed ready to conquer the world of entertainment. Yet before he could even buy a train ticket to New York, Uncle Sam sent him a draft notice. The first holiday season of World War II would be the young man's final one in Michigan for some time.

Several months before Christmas, as Al enjoyed his last days of civilian life, his father approached him.

"Al, you are now the pro. I want you to write the music for this year's card, and I will provide the lyrics."

The younger Burt immediately and enthusiastically accepted the task, then seemed to completely forget his promise. Even when his father handed him the new verses, Al just set them aside. Each day, an anxious Bates would inquire if the young man had started writing, and the answer would always be, "Not yet, but I'm going to get to it soon."

"My dad always put things off," Diane explained. "That was the way he was. So my grandfather kept pushing him and reminding him. Finally, in November, on the day the card was scheduled to go to the printer, he sat down to compose the music."

It took Al just fifteen minutes to write and arrange "O Christmas Cometh Caroling." It was a much different carol than had been placed on the Burt cards in the past.

"My grandfather loved the pomp and circumstance of Christmas," Diane pointed out. "His carols were very formal and anthem-like."

Bate's son had the heart of a jazz musician. While his father's music captured the mood found in old German and English anthems, Al embraced the essence and lightness of the American pop sounds. So "O Christmas Cometh Caroling" was a much different song than Bates had envisioned when he penned the words. Yet still the older man was almost as overjoyed with the carol's modern flowing music as he was in making the printing deadline. With America in the midst of a war, the 1942 edition of the Burt's family card, with its bright artwork and jazzy carol, was a very bright spot in what would be a dark Christmas for many families.

During the war, Burt played in the Army Air Force Band and traveled all over the globe lifting spirits with his musical talent. During those hectic days, he also fell in love, got married, and provided the original music for three more carols. In the years right after the war, Al and his new bride, Anne, continued to journey from coast to coast performing with a big band, but the couple still managed to find time to visit with Father Burt in Marquette, Michigan. Al also continued to team with his dad on the annual family Christmas carol.

"When my grandfather died in 1949," Diane explained, "Mom and Dad decided to carry on the tradition. Dad was not a lyricist, so he asked a close family friend, Wihla Hutson, to provide the poetry."

Wihla would become a vital link in creating the now-legendary Burt carols. A church organist, a songwriter, and an amateur arranger, she often spent the holidays with the Burt family. Her practice of writing Christmas poems and stuffing her verses into stockings was probably the inspiration that launched Bates Burt's original card-carol tradition. Like the elder Burt, Hutson felt that the best Christmas gifts came from the heart and echoed the spirit of the season.

"When my father asked Wihla to write the Christmas-card lyrics," Diane explained, "she agreed immediately. My dad and mom discussed what each wanted from the songs, and at that point the carols took on a slightly different flavor. My grandfather was always inspired by the pageantry of the season, as well as what they were doing in the church. Mom and Dad decided their cards would be about what was happening in their family. With that decided, Wihla and Dad then set a pattern of one year having a sacred carol and the next year a secular one. They also decided on having three verses in each new song."

Anne was pregnant and stayed home in Michigan when Al went back on the road that fall. For the woman who had always traveled with her husband, it would be both an exciting and lonely time. Though he wrote and called often, Anne deeply missed Al. Sensing the young woman's loneliness, Wihla Hutson became Anne's second mother and best friend. It would be Wihla who helped many long days and nights pass more quickly.

As the midwestern autumn gave way to the bitter cold of a Michigan winter, Wihla began to consider the message the new family would need on their first Christmas card. She was acutely aware of the events in the couple's life and wanted to pen something that would somehow share this with their friends. One night, a lonely Anne called Wihla and asked if they could meet for supper. Giving up her plans for the evening, the older woman drove thirty miles over snow-covered roads to a restaurant. Anne was overjoyed to see the woman walk in the eatery's door. Just seeing Wihla's smile seemed to brighten the pregnant woman's spirits.

That night as they ate, all Anne could talk about was how excited she and Al were over the coming baby. As the poet studied the younger woman's glowing face, a poem popped into her head. Those lyrics, coupled with one of Al's melodies, would become the centerpiece for the card that year. The card's carol was called "Sleep Baby." Yet it was a second set of verses, ones that were again inspired at this same dinner, that would become one of the most touching spiritual carols ever penned.

"That night," Diane continued, remembering the story Wihla later shared with her, "as she listened to Mom, Wihla took on the enthusiasm of being a new mother. In a sense Mom was imagining things that night through her unborn child's eyes. As they visited, Wihla noted that Mom even saw Jesus as a little child would see him."

Wihla was deeply touched as she looked at Anne in this new light. As they said their goodbyes and the older woman got back into her car to drive back to her home, Wihla's mind was crowded with thoughts of children. She realized that if she were a child in Africa she would see the world much differently than a child in the United States would. An African child would see Jesus as a black man. Then she realized that a Chinese child would see the Son of God with almond eyes, while an Indian child would see Jesus with dark hair and brown skin. As she never had before, Wihla grasped the concept of God's being a universal spirit. For the first time she realized that as

Jesus entered the heart of a child, that child would see him as being like them. And he really was, too.

Wihla eased the car to the side of the road. Pulling a pencil from her purse, Hutson turned on the car's dome light and began to quickly put her thoughts into a poem. The words flew from her heart so quickly she could barely jot them down. After concluding the final stanza, she read them over, said a prayer of thanks, and pulled back onto the highway.

Diane said, "My mom and dad didn't put 'Some Children See Him' on a card until 1951. In 1949 my birth was announced with 'Carol of Mothers,' or what is now called 'Sleep Baby.' In 1950 'Bright, Bright the Holly Berries' was the carol on the card. In fact, even though he had had the lyrics for almost two years, Dad didn't write the music to 'Some Children See Him' until just a few days before Mom had to have the 1951 cards printed."

When he finally decided to go to work, it took Al just twenty minutes to compose the new carol's music. That card, like those before it, was delivered on time. As Christmas passed and a new year began, the Burts settled into their normal routine, not expecting "Some Children See Him" ever to be sung except at future family holiday gatherings.

"My father was a very humble man," Diane said. "The carols were not the thrust of his musical life, just an endearing tradition that linked him to his faith and his family. Yet in 1952, as he finished up that year's card carol, he asked the Blue Reys to check the harmonies in 'Come, Dear Children.' "

The Blue Reys were a nationally known group of singers who traveled with Alvino Rey and his orchestra. Al had worked with the orchestra and the singers since right after World War II. Yet in all that time, he had never shared his Christmas music with them. As a group who had taken such hits as "Deep in the Heart of Texas" to the top of the charts, these men were not easy to impress. They listened very carefully to scores of different songs before deciding to record one. But because of their friendship with Al, they took a stab at his carol. They not only liked it, they were blown away. They immediately asked Burt if he had any more like this one. The composer then played several of his other holiday originals, including "Some Children See Him." The guys were so impressed they asked if they could perform a few of Burt's carols at the King Sisters' Christmas party.

Initially Al tried to dissuade the Blue Reys from using his work for the King Sisters' bash. After all, some of the biggest names in music always showed up at the party, and Burt thought those stars might view the singing of his songs as a pitch attempt. He felt this would put a commercial spin on the festivities that would be in poor taste. Yet as the Blue Reys would not give up, Al eventually gave in. Thanks to the performance at that party, Columbia Records took an interest in Burt's carols. A holiday album that came out in 1955 finally exposed the talents and faith of Alfred Burt to the world. Sadly, by the time the world first heard "Some Children See Him," the writer had lost a hard-fought battle with cancer.

"This song has become a very favorite carol of a lot of recording artists," Diane pointed out. "Andy Williams, Bing Crosby, Maureen McGovern, Kenny Loggins, Norma Zimmer, who was a part of the original carol recordings of Dad's songs, and so many others have put their stamp on it. It is still being recorded on Christmas albums by new artists each year."

Perhaps because of the missionary movement, this Al Burt composition is a part of many third-world Christmas celebrations. Maybe children around the globe embrace this simple carol because it presents Jesus as being so much like them. As the song says,

> *The children in each different place*
> *Will see the Baby Jesus' face*
> *Like theirs,*
> *But bright with heavenly grace.*

Historical events often unfold in random fashion, but in many cases it takes a seemingly unimportant action to give the world an unfathomable treasure. In a tiny town in the Middle East, a baby was born in a stable. Few noticed that child then, but now billions of all races celebrate his birth each December 25.

In 1843, an English nobleman named Sir Henry Cole did not have time to answer his December mail, so he sent out cards with a holiday verse. Thus began the custom of Christmas cards. Almost eighty years later an Episcopal priest put a new spin on Cole's annual tradition by writing a carol. Without these seemingly unconnected events, Albert Burt would never have written such songs as "The Star Carol," "We'll Dress the House," "This Is Christmas," "Caroling Caroling," or "Some Children See Him." And without these songs and the message that inspired them, the world would be a much darker place.

Caroling, Caroling

C hristmas in Hollywood is anything but white, so even though there are Santas on every corner, folks often have a tough time getting into the spirit of the season. December in Southern California does not conjure up holiday images that are depicted on cards, movies, or television. Rather than wearing huge wool coats, hats, and mufflers, the locals go on their sun-filled Christmas shopping missions in short-sleeved shirts and open-toed shoes. Sleds are replaced by skateboards, and evergreens by palm trees. So when California shoppers suddenly hear awe-inspiring harmonies and turn to see a group of eight carolers dressed in Victorian-era winter garb performing such numbers as "We'll Dress the House" or "Caroling, Caroling," they usually do a doubletake. After all, mufflers and long coats are as foreign in Los Angeles as snow. And yet each holiday season, the Caroling Company comes out in full winter regalia, creating through music and attire the atmosphere of a traditional snowy Christmas.

The founder and leader of the Caroling Company is a beautiful, energetic brunette blessed with an angelic voice with the power of a steam locomotive. Diane Burt loves the season as much as she relishes each moment of her life. For this Southern Californian, this really is the most wonderful time of the year. After all, when she sings carols, she is doing more than creating holiday magic for sun-drenched West Coast natives;

she is also continuing a Christmas tradition that spans three generations.

Performing original Christmas songs has been a part of the Burt family since 1922. It was during that holiday season Diane's grandfather, an Episcopal priest, composed an original holiday carol and included it in that year's Christmas cards. For the next thirty-two years, through wars, depressions, and good times and bad, first from the pen of Father Bates, and then later written by Diane's dad, Alfred Burt, the tradition of writing original carols and sending them out to friends and family at Christmas continued. In 1954, with the death of Alfred Burt, the cards and carols suddenly stopped, but the music lives on as Diane and her company continue sharing the sweet sounds of Christmas.

"The Caroling Company," Diane explained, "is an eight-voice ensemble organized to represent my father's carols in their original form, a cappella. Over the years, the members of the Caroling Company have become part of our family. It is safe to say that it wouldn't be Christmas without the carols or the Caroling Company."

Diane was just four years old when cancer took her father. She was far too young to understand his genius or understand how much those in the entertainment industry loved this singer, musician, composer, and arranger. While she sensed something special was happening during the final months of his life, and while she noted the constant influx of people who seemed to have Christmas on their minds even in the midst of a summer heat wave, she did not know that her father, mother, and an important element of the West Coast music industry were all rushing to bring Burt's holiday carols to the whole world.

This inspiration that would consume so much of Alfred's last months had been born some three decades before in Marquette, Michigan. In this area of vast virgin forests, tumbling streams, and long winters, the holidays came alive each year.

This is where Alfred had been born and raised, where he had learned the importance of the light of Christmas in church and through constant examples of sharing and giving. This is where Christmas had taken a great meaning for him and where thoughts of real peace consumed his goals for life. He thought of that peace often when serving in the military during World War II. His desire to bring that peace to others consumed him even after he married, rejoined civilian life, and moved to sunny Los Angeles. In the hustle and bustle of Hollywood, Burt found vast potential as a trumpet player and composer, but he also saw people in too much of a hurry to fully find any kind of meaning in their lives.

One of those who had heavily influenced Burt was the organist for his father's church. Wihla Hutson had been born at the turn of the century, so she was old enough to be Al's mother, and as a boy, Alfred looked at the unmarried woman as an aunt. But Wihla had become more than just a part of his family; she was also an inspiration. A college-trained musician, Hutson was the boy's mentor. She helped develop Al's passion for music. And as she composed her own songs, Wihla also encouraged the boy's desire to create original music.

Burt was playing jazz and arranging music for big bands in the late forties when he and Hutson began to collaborate on carols for the annual Burt Christmas cards. Though both had published music, neither considered their card carols anything more than holiday gifts for family and friends. That abruptly changed in 1953. Two different events would turn the Burt family upside down and pave the way for the world to hear some of the most beautiful Christmas music ever written.

In the late winter, Burt had been working long hours on a television show featuring Alvino Rey and the King Sisters. Finishing his arrangements for the network series, he then spent several weeks on the road with the Horace Heidt Orchestra. While he never complained, a persistent cough continued to drag him down. Finally, when he was unable to perform, he went into the hospital for tests. The diagnosis was lung cancer. There was no chance for a cure, and Al's life was now numbered in months, not years.

For Burt the news was heartbreaking in more ways than he could begin to fathom. After nine years of hard work establishing himself, he almost had achieved his dreams. He and his wife had a nice home, his daughter was so young, his career was just taking off, and his life in Hollywood had just then moved him into a spot where his music was being noted by the top talents in town. Orchestras wanted him to play for them, television producers were seeking his services as an arranger, and nightclub performers wanted him to help them with their acts. Now all that was over. He would never write the Broadway musical that had been a part of his dreams, never land a number-one hit on *Billboard*'s music charts, and never compose the score for a major motion picture. Worse yet, he would never grow old with his wife or get to see his daughter, Diane, grow up.

As Al came to grips with his cruel fate, he was convinced he would soon be forgotten. He believed his legacy would be little more than a grave and a tombstone. Other men, those who didn't have a deep faith, would have given up, maybe even taken their own lives. But rather than be despondent, rather than cry out in anger, Burt continued to reach out to others. He was determined that whatever days he had left would be the best ones of his life. He didn't want anyone to remember him as anything but happy.

Just before Christmas 1952, the Blue Reys, a nationally known singing group, had discovered one of Burt's annual Christmas card carols. They had happened on it when Alfred had asked the guys to help him check the harmonies of "Come Dear Children." The Blue Reys were taken by the carol they performed at the annual King Sisters' Christmas show. James

Conkling, the president of Columbia Records, heard that performance. The label executive was so moved he inquired if Alfred had written any more holiday songs. When James discovered Burt had penned an original carol each year since 1942, Conkling asked to review all of them. He was still in the process of studying the carols when he learned of the composer's illness.

From the moment he first played them, Conkling knew the songs were very good, but he had seen no reason to really push them until he discovered Burt was dying. Yet the carols James had been given would not fill up an entire album. Hesitantly, he approached Al's wife, Anne, explaining he needed four more carols for the project. He was hoping Burt had composed extras in the past that had not been used on the family cards. Sadly, he discovered that Burt had created only one new carol each year, and all of those were now in Conkling's hands. The last thing the record executive wanted to do was ask a dying man to spend his last few months working on music, but if the album was going to include just Burt's songs, more would have to be created.

While Conkling did not wish to bother Burt, Anne saw this dilemma as an answered prayer. This would give her husband's life focus. She immediately went to Al's bed and explained that for the album to be recorded, he would have to create four more Christmas songs. Though he was spending his days in a wheelchair, his voice raspy and his energy level down, the frail man seized the challenge with the vigor of an athlete. Though motivated like he had never before been, he knew he couldn't do the work all by himself. Picking up the phone, he called Wihla Hutson and asked the church organist for four more sets of lyrics.

"Wihla later told me," Diane recalled, "that all she needed was Al's request, and the words flowed so fast she could hardly write them down."

One of the sets of words Hutson created harkened back to Alfred Burt's childhood. It was a lyrical postcard of all the holiday ingredients that had made the man's childhood days in Michigan so very special. Even though he was fighting agonizing pain and struggling for each new breath, it took the composer only a short while to brilliantly score "Caroling, Caroling."

Just before Christmas 1953, with all four new songs completed, a volunteer chorus organized by the King Sisters, Buddy Cole, and Jimmy Joyce met in a North Hollywood church to do the initial taping for the album. Al was on hand, thrilled with each rendition these carolers created with his music. Partway through the session, when he finally listened to "Caroling, Caroling," it seemed the pain left his body and he was transported back to the carefree days of his youth. Christmas was alive again, and the peace of the season had completely enveloped the dying man.

"This is the happiest day of my life," he told his wife. Within a month and a half, Al would be gone.

The Columbia album of Burt's carols was released the next Christmas. The songs were not immediate hits. Few rushed out to purchase the album, and no other artists hit the studio to cut Al's songs. It seemed the songs would live on only at future family holiday gatherings. By the next Christmas, it seemed that even Columbia had lost interest in the project.

In a world of constantly changing tastes, Al was soon forgotten by all except his closest friends. Yet one of those friends, a man who had been dynamically impacted by the musical perfection that came from the man called "The Professor," would not allow the carols to die. Ralph Carmichael, who would become one of the founders of contemporary Christian music and compose such hymns as "The Savior Is Waiting," took "Caroling, Caroling" to Nat King Cole's record producer. Cole, whose version of Mel Torme's "Christmas Song" had made him one of the most beloved voices of the holiday season, was cutting an album of holiday music. Carmichael wanted one of Burt's songs to be featured.

On a summer day in 1961, Carmichael pled his case, but the producer didn't even allow him to play a demo of "Caroling, Caroling." He informed Carmichael that Cole's project would be filled with only traditional carols and Nat's classic "Christmas Song." They didn't want anything new on the album. As Ralph picked up Burt's song and sadly walked toward the office door, his eyes met Nat's. Cole smiled, stood up, grabbed the demo, and put it on the record player. One spin was all it took to convince Cole that "Caroling, Caroling" was one of the most spirited holiday songs he had ever heard. Cole's hit recording of that Burt song would help open the door for scores of artists to discover all of Alfred's Christmas music. The legacy was now assured.

"He heard things others could not hear," Diane explained. "Dad was a pianist, an arranger, a composer, a trumpet player, and a singer, and he understood music from the inside out.

"The last songs he wrote were all up-tempo. Even though he was dying, he wanted the family's mindset to be happy. My mom told me that when he was working on 'Caroling, Caroling,' it reminded him of his Christmases in Michigan. He thought again of the sleigh rides, sitting on bales of hay in Pontiac, and the other wonderful things of Christmas as a child."

While "Caroling, Caroling" would have been fabulous and timeless if it had included only those elements of holidays long ago, Wihla Hutson knew that for Alfred, Christmas meant something more than the secular images seen on the streets. In the song's final verse the theme shifts from decorations and merriment to a star and a baby.

> *Lo, the king of heav'n is born*
> *Christmas bells are ringing.*

"Dad told Wihla that even though each song could speak of the Christmas of the secular world," Diane explained, "they always had to go back to the reason for the season. They had to honor Christ's birth."

In his first Christmas card after the end of World War II, Alfred Burt's father had written, "The secret of joy out of sorrow and gain out of loss is all there in the message of Christmas."

In February of 1954, Alfred Burt died assured by the message found in the Christmases he knew and the ones he shared with others through his music. He never realized his songs would be welcomed in concert halls, churches, schools, on radio and television, and in homes around the world. He never realized his carols would become some of the most meaningful elements of the season. He never dreamed his goal of helping to bring a spiritual peace to the world would be seen by his daughter. Yet how proud he would have been to have Diane and the Caroling Company continue his tradition of sharing through song the real message of Christmas with others each holiday season. Thanks to "Caroling, Caroling," even those in Southern California can feel the cold snowy breeze and the bright star of hope that are so much a part of an ideal holiday season.

THE STAR CAROL

O n February 5, 1954, Alfred Burt sensed the end was coming. Though just thirty-three years old, Burt was in the final hours of his fight with cancer. In spite of the fact the horrific illness had robbed him of his energy and strength and left him in agonizing pain, the gentle man resolutely turned his attention to the final song he would ever compose. With a grim determination he took another look at the musical score he had written for Wihla Hutson's lyrics. It seemed right, but he wasn't sure. Too weak to press the keys of the piano that sat before him, Burt patiently waited for the arrival of his friend, musical arranger Jimmy Joyce.

For more than ten months Al had fought cancer with every fiber of his being. He had suffered through countless cobalt treatments and helplessly watched as the disease ate away at his body. He had dealt with the panic brought on by having to fight for each breath as the cancer invaded his lungs. He had seen the horror on friends' faces as they viewed his deterioration. He had heard the whispered predictions that he would not live to see Thanksgiving or Christmas, and yet remarkably he had made it through those two holidays and beyond.

Two things had driven him to struggle for every extra moment of life. The first was his daughter, a child too young to understand what was happening to him. He desperately wanted Diane to think of him in a positive way and to remember her

89

childhood as a happy one. He wanted to make such a dynamic impression on the little girl that whenever she thought of her father, it would be with a smile. Thus, in the face of great agony, he spent time with his only child. He listened to her stories, smiled at her jokes, and found ways to make her laugh.

The other thing driving the man to fight through each day was a need to finish composing four songs. That was how many Columbia Records needed to release an album of his Christmas music. So, even a month and a half after Christmas, Burt pushed on, trying to put the spirit of all the holidays he would miss into this last project.

Wihla Hutson, who had been a musical mentor to him since youth, had carefully crafted four sets of lyrics. Each was unique and reflected a different facet of how Al viewed the holidays. Because of Burt's positive nature, each of the new songs was uplifting, with the verses flowing together in ways that were bright and happy. Thus, just reading over Hutson's words lifted the very tired man's spirit. Yet even the spiritual message found in Wihla's contribution could not push back the inevitable end that was coming.

Death had now begun to etch its portrait into Al's face. His skin was now drawn, his color almost ashen, his lips tinted with a gray cast. Yet as he again reviewed his arrangement, his eyes still possessed an energy and expression that fought against death's clutches. He had work to do, a goal to reach, and an appointment to keep. He had to finish the song that would become the last one ever placed on a Burt family Christmas card.

Over the past few months, Al had penned the music for "O Harken Ye," "We'll Dress the House," and "Caroling, Caroling." Now, as he studied the notes he had scribbled on the line and staffs in front of him, he believed his work was almost finished. Yet he would have to hear his friend and musical arranger Jimmy Joyce play it before he would know for sure. Burt was still carefully reviewing one segment of his new carol when Joyce finally walked into the room.

Joyce had visited Al daily for some weeks now, trying to take care of any needs that Burt, his wife, Anne, or their small daughter, Diane, might have. But in spite of the fact it had been less than twenty-four hours since he had last seen him, the close friend was still shocked by how much the frail man's condition had deteriorated. He looked a decade older and much weaker. Yet as their eyes met, Joyce realized his old friend was still inside that feeble body. Even in the midst of life's last throes, Burt's zest for living still somehow hung on.

Al pushed the arrangement to his new song toward Jimmy. No words were exchanged as the musician picked it up and walked over to the piano. As Joyce sat down, Anne Burt studied her husband's anxious expression. She sensed he wanted to hear the song even more than she did. He had to know if his musical creation lived up to the incredible lyrics Wihla had written for him.

Joyce glanced over the score and then began to play. Suddenly a deeply moving melody filled the room with the joy of all the future Christmases Al would never know. Hutson's spiritual message had been wrapped in a musical package as hauntingly simple but strikingly beautiful as "Silent Night." It was timeless, perfectly capturing the glorious mood of the first Christmas, as well as the eternal spirit that should be a part of every holiday season. When Jimmy finished the final notes of "The Star Carol," the room was hushed.

"It's beautiful," Anne finally sighed, tears filling her eyes.

"The most perfect thing you have ever written," echoed Jimmy.

Yet even as those two celebrated the new composition, Al shook his head. It didn't sound quite right to him. So with a lifted hand, he halted the praise and asked Joyce to replay the number.

"At that time," Diane explained, "my dad was a physical wreck. Yet in spite of that, he was still very particular about his music. Jimmy played it through, and Jimmy told him again it was perfect. But my dad felt something was not right."

Al asked for the music. Taking the sheet into his thin fingers, he picked up a pencil and changed one note in the tenor harmonization. He then handed it back to Joyce and waited to hear it played one more time. After Jimmy had finished, he and Anne looked anxiously toward Burt.

"Now," he sighed, "it is finished."

Long after the piano had grown silent and Joyce had left, the strains of "The Star Carol" still filled the Burt home. From its beginning line, "Long years ago on a deep winter night," to its closing, "And when the stars in the heavens I see, ever and always I'll think of Thee," even in the midst of February, the message of the perfect Christmas rang throughout the house.

Later that night, Al found the strength to eat supper, watch a few cartoons with Diane, and then see the little girl off to bed. An hour later he sat in his wheelchair, lost in thought, when Anne appeared before him. She had made one of Al's favorite Christmas treats, hot chocolate and strawberry shortcake. Silently he sipped on the cocoa and took a few bites of the dessert. As she looked over at her husband, the woman knew that he had accomplished what he had to do. The race was over.

Overcome with grief, Anne excused herself and rushed outside. Alone in the yard, she looked up and found herself under the most incredible star-filled sky she had ever seen. No matter which way she looked, it seemed every one of heaven's lights was shining directly upon their home. Inspired by the display, Anne returned to Al's side.

"Anne," he said as she sat down before him, "will you do two things for me?"

The woman nodded.

"Take care of our daughter and please take care of my music."

The next morning, less than twelve hours after hearing his last carol for a final time, Al died. In the ultimate irony, a messenger from Columbia Records arrived at the Burt home a few minutes later with a signed contract to produce an album of Al's carols.

For every Christmas since 1922, the Burt family had mailed to friends and family an original carol printed on the front of the card. The first twenty years the songs had been penned by the family patriarch, Bates Burt. In 1942, just before he entered the U.S. Army Air Force, Al took over that creative element. The younger Burt's first contribution was "O Christmas Cometh Caroling." "The Star Carol" would be the song that put an end to the tradition.

"It was the most beautiful of all the cards," Diane recalled. "Columbia Records gave my mom the picture for the front. It really looked like me. Columbia printed the cards and used them as an announcement for the new album, 'The Christmas Mood.' The song that framed the card was my dad's final work, 'The Star Carol.' It was my mom's and my way of sharing Dad's work and his life one more time."

"The Christmas Mood" did not make a big splash in the music world. There were simply too many new musical holiday offerings for Burt's carols to gain any airplay. Plus few wanted to push songs written by someone who had just died. And though she had promised to take care of his music, that included Anne Burt.

"Dad didn't know if anyone would buy the record," Diane remembered. "He just wanted it out. He needed that to happen to complete his life. At that time, the last thing Mom wanted was to open up her life to the world. So she didn't want the carols to become well known because she didn't want to talk about Dad's death from cancer. And she knew that is what people would dwell on. She just wanted people to listen to the music for the music. At that time she was willing to put them in a drawer and bring them out at Christmas for family and leave it at that."

Even though "The Christmas Mood" did not sell well in 1954, the songs were too special to simply fade away. Buddy Cole, the producer who put the finishing notes on the album, was one who would not let the world forget Al Burt and his music. Though Cole had already established himself as one of the best-known musicians in Hollywood, the impact Al had made on his life pushed him to use his contacts to keep the carols in front of the world. Realizing the great spiritual impact found within the songs' lyrics and arrangements, four years after Al's death, Buddy took what he viewed as the most dynamic of the Burt carols to one of the most beloved stars of early television, Tennessee Ernie Ford.

Unlike many of the popular music artists of the era, Ford was not afraid of recording music with great spiritual overtones. Though he had started his career as a comedian and scored a monster hit with "Sixteen Tons," Ernie's gospel recordings had become the centerpiece of his career. Thus, when he heard Burt's "The Star Carol" for the first time, the deep impact of the song's biblical message, combined with the song's most beautiful melody, touched Ford as no other carol ever had. He sensed the song was an answer to his prayer to put more of Christ back into the American Christmas.

On October 20, 1958, Capital Records released Ford's first album of holiday classics. Every cut on the new record reflected the biblical story of Jesus. Along with such historic carols as "Silent Night" and "O Little Town of Bethlehem," Ernie added three contemporary cuts: Burt's "O Harken Ye," "Some Children See Him," and "The Star Carol."

Capital was so awed by Ford's performance of Burt's "The Star Carol," the label made the carol the new album's title cut.

Just as it was being released to radio and in stores, Ford introduced it on his network television show.

"We had been told that Ernie was going to sing it that night," Diane remembered, "and Buddy Cole had invited us to his house to watch the show. My mother was deeply moved by Ernie's performance. Immediately after hearing it, she sent Ernie a telegram that said, 'Thank you and bless your little carol-pickin' heart.' This was, of course, due to Ernie's catch-saying, "Bless your little pea-pickin' heart."

Ford's "The Star Carol" became one of the most requested songs of the new Christmas season. It remained Ernie's signature holiday number for the remainder of his life.

The release and acceptance of "The Star Carol" changed Anne's perception of her husband's legacy. Whereas she had once been content for his carols to be an important element of the Burt family Christmas, now she understood how much they could mean to the whole world. Ford's recording the carol and making it a holiday hit also caused the woman to appreciate that one of Al's personal dreams was being realized. He was now recognized by the industry he wanted so badly to be a part of.

Few songs have ever captured the meaning of the season like "The Star Carol" has. And though the lyrics are obviously inspired, it is the music which carries this song, sets its tone, and makes it so popular with both recording artists and the public. That is why scores of recording artists, plus thousands of churches around the world, have embraced Al's final carol.

For most people, February 5, 1954, was a day when the only reminders of Christmas could be found in the arrival of some holiday bills. Though it would also be the last day of Al Burt's life, it was Christmas one more time at his home. And what a final Christmas day it was! Thanks to this composer's drive to finish a song, the world took a second look at the meaning of a star that once shown brightly over a manger in Bethlehem.

Bathed in the spotlight of that star was not just the subject of Burt's last carol but the Lord who inspired and shaped each day of Al's life. "The Star Carol" was finished on the final day of Al Burt's life, but it paved the way for the man's gifts of faith to be shared with the whole world each Christmas season.

Come, Thou
Long-Expected Jesus

Most Christmas songs are reserved only for the advent season. It is a fact that churches and radio stations rarely offer up a holiday tune during any time but the months of November and December. Yet one revered carol, based, ironically, on an Old Testament Scripture, has escaped the bounds of the seasonal timetable and is often used as a hymn during every season of the year. To accomplish this remarkable feat, it would take a man who composed more than seven thousand hymns, scores of which are still sung today. Yet in spite of his incredible contributions to the Christian music world, this revered writer once suffered great doubt and struggled to find direction and purpose in his life.

Charles Wesley was born on December 18, 1707, the eighteenth child of Samuel and Susanna Wesley. At fifteen months the boy almost died in a church fire. If a maid had not rescued the tiny child, future hymnals around the globe would have been robbed of some of their most celebrated songs. Perhaps a bit of the heat of that inferno provided the spark that later fueled Wesley's remarkable life. But before the creative Charles could take wing with works that have inspired millions, he would have to come to see his own inadequacies.

Charles and his brother, John, were given the best education available in England. Both finished college determined to become ministers. At the age of twenty-two, Charles would band together with other students of the gospel and launch the Methodist movement. Ironically, it would be John, who joined the "Holy Club" after the foundation of the denomination had been organized, who would become the leader of this new Protestant band.

In 1735, Charles accompanied John on the mission to the new colony of Georgia. The brothers journeyed to America to bring Old World gospel to the colonists. Having led sheltered and privileged lives, they were no match for the demands of the New World. They won few friends, earned little respect, and began to doubt their own call to the clergy. Within a year, a defeated and disillusioned Charles returned to England. Confused, Wesley began a spiritual quest that saw him studying the words of mystics like William Law as well as trying to understand the missionary zeal of groups like the Moravians.

Charles continued to drift until he experienced another life-changing event. A severe attack of pleurisy almost cost him his life and confined him to a bed for months. While unable even to take care of himself, Wesley reconnected with God. After reading Isaiah 40:1, he wrote, "I now found myself at peace with God, and rejoiced in hope of loving Christ. I went to bed still sensible of my own weakness, yet confident of Christ's protection."

The next day Wesley jotted down this verse:

> *Where shall my wondering soul begin?*
> *How shall I all to heaven aspire?*
> *A slave redeemed from death and sin,*
> *A brand plucked from eternal fire!*
> *How shall I equal triumphs raise*
> *Or sing my great Deliverer's praise?*

A year later a then-healthy Charles would complete his sick-bed musings by writing "Oh for a Thousand Tongues to

Come, thou long-expected Jesus,
Born to set thy people free;
From our fears and sins release us,
Let us find our rest in thee.
Israel's strength and consolation,
Hope of all the earth thou art;
Dear desire of every nation,
Joy of every longing heart.
Born thy people to deliver,
Born a child, and yet a King,
Born to reign in us for ever,
Now thy gracious kingdom bring.
By thine own eternal Spirit,
Rule in all our hearts alone:
By thine all-sufficient merit,
Raise us to thy glorious throne. Amen.

Sing." This song not only would launch the career of the world's most renowned composer of hymns but would also become the minister's testimony, one that is heard by more people today than even during Wesley's lifetime. Over the course of the next few years, the emboldened writer would pen such gospel classics as "Christ the Lord Is Risen Today," "Hark! The Herald Angels Sing," "Jesus Lover of My Soul," and "Love Divine All Loves Excelling." Though thought of as just a standard worship hymn today, for many years the latter was considered one of England and America's most popular Christmas songs.

While today "Love Divine" is no longer used during the holidays, "Come, Thou Long-Expected Jesus" has emerged as Wesley's second most popular Christmas carol behind "Hark! The Herald Angels Sing." Charles wrote the song around the age of forty, and though this hymn dealt with the birth of Jesus, the composer was actually inspired by Haggai 2:7 to compose this seasonal carol: "And I will shake all nations, and the desire of all nations shall come: and I will fill this house with glory saith the Lord of hosts."

After reading these words, Wesley began to consider what Jesus' birth meant to the world's people. The minister lived in a time when many were suffering in hunger and poverty. There were orphans all around him. The distinction between the classes was distinct and large. He also knew a world in which slavery was allowed. It seemed that in the more than 1,700 years since the Lord had come, humanity had improved little, if at all.

As Wesley considered the plight of so many in the world and then thought of Jesus' birth, a hopeful thought consumed him. With great anticipation he found himself looking forward toward the second coming of Christ, desiring to see that with as much zeal as the writer of Haggai had looked forward to the Lord's birth. And like the man who wrote down those words in the Old Testament, Wesley realized he would have to be patient. God's timing would take precedence over man's desires.

As he thought of what the birth meant in the eyes of those looking forward to it, Wesley began to jot down the lines of "Come, Thou Long-Expected Jesus." Much more than a babe in the manger, the Jesus Charles wrote about was the adult king who came to set people free. He was the fulfilling of prophecy and the answer to the problems not only of every man, woman, and child, but of each of the earth's nations. Though Wesley's lyrics acknowledged and emphasized the mighty power of God, his words also embraced the loving nature of Jesus. While it was the power that would deliver the world from sin, it was God's love that would ultimately change us into being more like Jesus. When he finished "Come, Thou Long-Expected Jesus," Wesley had perfectly married power and love.

Published in 1744, "Come, Thou Long-Expected Jesus" was sung to several different melodies during its first few years before most hymnals finally assigned Wesley's lyrics to a tune written by Rowland Huw Prichard. The Welsh-born Prichard was an untrained musician who led singing in his Bala, Wales, church. A worker at the Welsh Flannel Manufacturing Company's mills, Prichard hardly seemed a man of the stature needed to compose music suitable for lyrics penned by Charles Wesley. Yet the loom-tender's dynamic "Hyfrydol" has proven so uplifting it has been married to not just "Come, Thou Long-Expected Jesus" but scores of other spiritual verses as well.

In 1788, at the age of eighty-one, Wesley was on his deathbed. The old man was now so weak he could not lift his hand to write. With what little breath he could muster, he called his wife, Sally, to his side and dictated his last verse:

> *In age and feebleness extreme,*
> *Who shall a helpless worm redeem?*
> *Jesus, my only hope Thou art,*

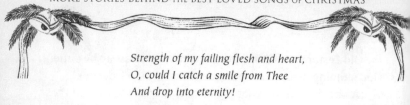

Strength of my failing flesh and heart,
O, could I catch a smile from Thee
And drop into eternity!

When he concluded his final thoughts, the great hymn writer finally had the personal experience of living out the last line in his great Christmas carol "Come, Thou Long-Expected Jesus." As soon as he drew his final breath, he surely rose to see the glorious throne of the Lord.

During the minister's life, Jesus had come to Wesley often. The writer had known God's presence in good times and bad. He had seen the birth of Christ through the eyes of children in his church as well as writers in the Old Testament. He had been inspired by those who had everything, as well as those who had nothing. And best of all, he kept none of these revelations to himself but shared them then, and continues to share them now, through his glorious hymns. Charles Wesley's words were so inspired that we still sing "Come, Thou Long-Expected Jesus" not only for Christmas but all year round.

It's Beginning to Look
a Lot Like Christmas

*I*t's Beginning to Look a Lot Like Christmas" joined together two of the most successful musicians of the last century. While this Christmas song brought both satisfaction and acclaim to both men's careers and still uplifts spirits each holiday season, their fame would have been assured even without it. But Christmas is always so much better when Perry Como's voice is heard singing Meredith Wilson's classic "It's Beginning to Look a Lot Like Christmas."

"It's Beginning to Look a Lot Like Christmas" sprang from a mind that had been creative since childhood. Born in Mason City, Iowa, in 1902, even as a small boy Meredith Wilson showed signs of incredible musical talent. Migrating east as a teen, he would study at what is now the Julliard School of Music. After he completed his studies in 1921, he would take his flute and perform with John Philip Sousa's world-famous marching band. Two years later he would become a vital force in the New York Philharmonic Orchestra. Wilson would stay with this esteemed group until 1929, when he moved to San Francisco to begin writing for a hot new medium.

In California, Wilson was the concert director for KFRC radio. His talent didn't go unnoticed by the networks for long. A few years later NBC brought the young man to Hollywood, where he not only composed and arranged a great deal of the music heard on the network's many radio series but also penned songs for movies such as *The Great Dictator* and *The Little Foxes*. Though few Americans knew Meredith Wilson's name, by 1940 almost everyone had heard his work.

After a stint in the service during World War II, Meredith returned to composing. Digging into a seemingly inexhaustible vault of inspired ideas, Wilson spun out such classics as "You and I," "May the Good Lord Bless and Keep You," and "Till There Was You." Yet he wasn't satisfied just writing hits. He longed for a place where he could use his full range of God-given talents. So while Hollywood offered Wilson success and security, it was Broadway that beckoned. While it might have been a risk to return to New York, it would prove to be on the stage that Wilson's greatest work would be realized.

During the fifties and sixties Meredith Wilson became known as "the Music Man." Creating such Broadway classics as *The Unsinkable Molly Brown* and *The Music Man*, two of the most beloved musicals of all time, Wilson was hot. Awards came to him almost as easily as did his inspiration. During the fifties, he was an entertainment giant! Still, often lost in the body of Wilson's inspired and incredibly successful work was a Broadway musical called *Here's Love*.

In *Here's Love* the composer had taken the hit Hollywood movie *Miracle on 34th Street* and turned it into a musical play. It would run for almost a year on the Great White Way, then be all but forgotten. Yet because one of the play's featured musical numbers embraced the hope and joy of Christmas like few songs ever had, a bit of Wilson's work would live on after the show closed.

While it may not have won a Tony or Grammy, like some of Wilson's other hits, "It's Beginning to Look a Lot Like Christmas" was a song that wrapped the special imagery of a season into a beautiful musical present. In truth, this song probably couldn't have been written in Hollywood. The West Coast environment simply wasn't right for the inspiration. Yet with Santas on every corner, snowflakes falling, bells ringing, and bundled-up kids spying into every frosty storefront window, New York City was a ready source for any writer willing to stop and notice the world around him. Wilson did more than note the activities of the days before Christmas; he put his observations onto paper.

With upbeat lyrics, Meredith Wilson painted vivid but simple imagery: toy displays, holiday decorations, and the emotions of all those caught up in the spirit of the holiday. In his lyrics, the faces of children and adults could easily be seen, as could the special presents that made up Santa's long list. Yet even as wonderful as all the merriment of the season was, nothing could compare to the joy of being home with the family for Christmas day. From carol singing to snow-covered trees, "It's Beginning to Look a Lot Like Christmas" had it all. This song was magical, but buried in a musical that was never brought to the screen, it was also almost lost.

Born ten years after Wilson, Perry Como, the seventh son of a seventh son, was a satisfied barber until he heard the voice of Bing Crosby. From that day on, he sang in his shop, fulfilling customer's requests for trims and tunes. Finally, after several years of barbershop concerts, a friend convinced Perry to put down his clippers and audition with Freddy Carlone's dance band. The barber won the spot.

From 1933 through 1943, Como toured the country with two different bands but had little impact on the entertainment world. No record companies came calling and no radio networks offered him a spot on their variety shows. Then, in the midst of World War II, just as he was negotiating a lease for his own barbershop, he got an unexpected offer from CBS to star in a New York–based radio show. Within weeks Como had also landed a contract with RCA Victor Records. Two years later Perry would be a household name as his "Till the End of Time" topped the charts for ten weeks. In 1948, he would leave radio and begin a long run as a TV star.

When he heard the Broadway show tune "It's Beginning to Look a Lot Like Christmas," Como was a holiday recording veteran, having already scored on the charts with two Christmas songs, "Winter Wonderland" and a cover of Irving Berlin's "White Christmas." Perry, who had cut several Broadway tunes in the past, was immediately drawn to the upbeat number. His voice, which often seemed to dance in the air, seemed perfectly suited for Wilson's melody. Using a trio, the Fontane Sisters, as his backup, the singing barber cut and released "It's Beginning to Look a Lot Like Christmas" in 1951. The song would ultimately become the big hit of the holiday season, a Como signature number, and one of the most recognized and popular modern Christmas musical offerings.

The rich but simple lyrics and uplifting tune of "It's Beginning to Look a Lot Like Christmas" probably did more to capture the real joy of an American Christmas than any other popular holiday standard. "White Christmas" was a tale of unfulfilled longing; "I'll Be Home for Christmas" was a song that mournfully spoke of a Christmas spent far away from home; and "Pretty Paper" was the story of a man left out of the celebration altogether. Yet in Meredith Wilson's "It's Beginning to Look a Lot Like Christmas," the happiness and wonder of the season were fully realized. This song offered peace and hope because it convinced listeners everywhere that things really were beginning to look not only a lot like Christmas but also like the Christmas of everyone's dreams.

THE COVENTRY CAROL

When Herod realized that he had been outwitted by the Magi, he was furious, and he gave orders to kill all the boys in Bethlehem and its vicinity who were two years old and under, in accordance with the time he had learned from the Magi. Then what was said through the prophet Jeremiah was fulfilled:

> A voice is heard in Ramah,
>> weeping and great mourning,
> Rachel weeping for her children
>> and refusing to be comforted,
> because they are no more.

—Matthew 2:16–18

These three verses from Matthew would seem a strange place to find inspiration for one of the oldest and most moving English Christmas songs. Yet in 1534, after reading this passage, Robert Croo composed what is now known as "The Coventry Carol." In a very real sense this unique holiday offering stands as one of the most beloved and misunderstood of all Christmas carols. Written as a small part of a presentation on the story of Jesus, for centuries "The Coventry Carol" has been taken out of context. The writer never intended the song to stand alone. It was only a small segment of a much larger narrative. Yet as a live presentation on a dark English evening proved, this number was so powerful that the peasant people of Coventry, England, never forgot it. Long after the musical it was taken from had been lost, the mothers of this village continued to sing "The Coventry Carol" to their children.

Today, in a world filled with electronic media and dynamic special effects, few stage productions have the power to take our breath away. In fact we are rarely awed by much of anything. Yet in the Middle Ages, perspectives were much different. Live performances by professional actors often left people astounded. For years they'd speak of what they had witnessed. In some cases the plays themselves changed the lives of those who saw them. Certainly this was the case with the musical that gave birth to "The Coventry Carol."

In the 1500s, English villages came alive whenever a traveling drama show came to town. These musical presentations provided rare entertainment for the working class of the period. When a troupe of actors arrived, a town's business would stop and shops would close. When they heard the news, farmers rushed out of their fields and their wives put off their chores. As enterprising vendors set up shop hawking food and drink, many families arrived early just to grab a spot near the stage. And what a stage it was. The actors performed on a bilevel platform mounted on wheels and pulled by horses or oxen. The lower level of the mobile theater was hidden behind curtains and served as a dressing chamber. The upper level consisted of a wooden floor. On the day of a performance, a backdrop was raised behind the second level, and the top deck would become the centerpiece of the performance. The fact that it was elevated allowed good viewing from both the front and the back of the village square. It also made the play a bigger-than-life event.

On a crisp evening in 1534, in Coventry, England, as hundreds gathered to watch the *Pageant of the Shearmen and Tailors,*

Lully, lullay, Thou little tiny Child,
By, by, lully, lullay.
O sisters too, how may we do,
For to preserve this day
This poor Youngling for Whom we sing
By, by, lully, lullay?
Herod the king, in his raging,
Charged he hath this day
His men of might, in his own sight,
All young children to slay.
That woe is me, poor Child for Thee!
And ever morn and day
For Thy parting neither say nor sing,
By, by, lully, lullay.
Lully, lullay, Thou little tiny Child,
By, by, lully, lullay.

there would be a moment in the production that would not just make its temporary mark on the audience but forever become a part of Christmas lore. Certainly the play's writer, Robert Cros, could not have predicted the impact of that one song, nor could any of the performers, yet something almost magical happened during the one facet of the performance that brought the gospel to life and branded an often-forgotten part of the Christmas story deeply into the hearts of the people of Coventry.

The *Pageant of the Shearmen and Tailors* was a mystery play. At this time, mystery did not mean the play was a "whodunit." Rather, these were productions that took their inspiration from the events of the four Gospels of the New Testament. For the audiences — made up of men and women who didn't own a copy of the Bible, who couldn't read, and who attended church services conducted only in Latin, a language they did not understand — these English-language presentations brought God's Word to life in a fashion they could finally understand. The crowds always sat in rapt attention, taking in each facet of the plays in a mood that embraced a real sense of wonder and worship.

Two-thirds of the way into the *Pageant of the Shearmen and Tailors*, it was announced that Herod was going to kill all the male children under the age of two in order to make sure the baby known as Jesus did not live to take his place as King of the Jews. The audience was probably shocked by this announcement. Most had never heard this part of the Christmas story. As the crowd contemplated Herod's lethal proclamation, a group of women holding babies appeared on the stage. As soldiers searched for the newborn boys, the women sang a soft and gentle lullaby trying to keep their babies from crying out and thus being discovered and slain.

Watching loving mothers attempt to protect innocent children made a dramatic impact on those in Coventry that night. Long after the professional actors had finished their performances, packed their wagons, and left, the people of the town continued to speak of that terrifying moment in the play. Hence the song those women performed that night in the *Pageant of the Shearmen and Tailors* was adopted as a lullaby by many mothers in the community. As it was passed down from generation to generation, the link to the story of Herod was forgotten by most. It was now just a lullaby. As such it became such a commonly sung tune in the town that it was known simply as "The Coventry Carol." Yet though the song was no longer associated with Herod's orders, the children killed by the king were not forgotten. The story lived on.

Perhaps it was because so many families had experienced the death of a child during the late Middle Ages that the story of the slaughter of the innocents took strong root in England. Many, including leaders of the church, vowed not to forget the unnamed boys who had died by the soldiers' swords. Even in the days before 1840, when few celebrated a religious Christmas, churches held special services on December 28 to remember the children Herod had ordered killed. To this day there are some places in Europe where the Feast of the Innocents is still observed, but few now know its tie to "The Coventry Carol."

The only known manuscript of the *Pageant of the Shearmen and Tailors* was destroyed in a fire in 1879. Hence the old mystery play is now all but forgotten. Yet the Christmas lullaby that so moved the people of Coventry and was saved by the mothers of the town lived on. After hundreds of years of being orally passed down, in 1878 it was finally published in *Christmas Carols New and Old*. As this was the dawning of the age of caroling, the soft and melodic song became popular with the holiday street singers of the late 1880s.

Today it seems strange that a song about the loss of so many innocent lives is the inspiration for one of the oldest English carols still sung. Yet this cherished holiday lullaby, set in a minor chord, is a haunting reminder of the power and fear that even kings felt when they heard that God's Son had been born. What the people of Coventry must have realized that first night was that "The Coventry Carol" was more than just a tribute to the sacrifice of the mothers of that first Christmas. It was also a tribute to God himself for giving his Son to save all the earth's people. And that is why the carol lives on!

HERE COMES SANTA CLAUS
(RIGHT DOWN
SANTA CLAUS LANE)

*I*n the late twenties, Gene Autry was working as a telegraph operator at a train depot in Sapula, Oklahoma, when a waiting passenger noted a guitar leaning up against a wall behind young Autry's desk. "Do you play that thing?" the man asked.

When Gene humbly acknowledged that he did, the passenger plopped down in a chair, leaned back against a wall, and said, "Well, let's hear something."

Though he was living in the wide open spaces of the rural Southwest, the telegraph operator was no stranger to audiences. He had been singing in church since he was old enough to stand and playing at local fairs and dances for more than ten years. He knew hundreds of songs, but as a fan of country music star Jimmie Rogers, Gene picked one of the "Blue Yodeler's" hits for this performance.

After listening to the number, the stranger got up from his chair, stuck out his hand, and declared, "You're pretty good. I am proud to meet you. My name is Will Rogers." A few minutes later Gene and Will dueted on "The Ballad of Casey Jones." They continued to visit and sing until Rogers's train arrived. As

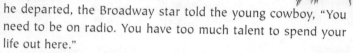

he departed, the Broadway star told the young cowboy, "You need to be on radio. You have too much talent to spend your life out here."

Will Rogers inspired Gene Autry to take his guitar and migrate east. Unfortunately, Gene's timing couldn't have been worse. He landed in New York just as the Great Depression hit the whole country. Discouraged and broke, he returned to Oklahoma only to find things were worse there than in the city. Catching a ride back east, Autry lived hand to mouth for a few months, then latched onto a record deal that would not only land him a radio show on WLS in Chicago but eventually give him a ticket to Hollywood and fame.

Other cowboys had sung in motion pictures before Gene, but he was by far the best. Making films that appealed to kids, Autry reeled off a long string of hit movies and records, including "That Silver-Haired Daddy of Mine" and "Back in the Saddle Again." By the late thirties, the former telegraph operator was a real star. He was also the hero of millions of American kids.

A part of Gene's charm lay in his character. Others might have played good guys on the screen, but Autry was one in real life. He not only wrote this "Cowboy Oath," often reciting it in his movies and on radio, but he also lived it in real life.

> He must not take unfair advantage of an enemy.
> He must never go back on his word.
> He must always tell the truth.
> He must always be gentle with children, elderly people,
>   and animals.
> He must not possess racially or religiously intolerant ideas.
> He must help people in distress.
> He must be a good worker.
> He must respect women, parents, and his nation's laws.
> He must neither drink nor smoke.
> He must be a patriot.

Autry's charm and talent would make him a millionaire. Yet success would not change or tarnish him. Largely due to his honesty on screen and off, he became one of the most revered men in America. Gene was so selfless, it came as no surprise when, less than a month after Pearl Harbor was bombed, prompting U.S. involvement in World War II, Autry enlisted in the Army Air Corps. He would serve as a commander in Burma. In battle he proved as courageous as the character he played in the movies.

Returning home after the war, Gene discovered that kids still wanted heroes. Gladly donning boots and a white hat, he again galloped across the silver screen, thrilling and teaching the youngsters who followed his every move. Gene the cowboy icon was so popular that when he appeared in person at rodeos, fairs, or theaters, he was often mobbed by those seeking to shake his hand.

In 1946, Gene was one of the special guests in the Hollywood Christmas parade. Riding his prized mount Champion, Autry was overwhelmed by the response of those who lined the parade route. As far as he could see, children were jumping up and down, pointing their fingers, screaming, and saluting. He couldn't believe how excited they were to see him. As he rode past one vocal youngster, Autry waved and smiled, but when the boy didn't acknowledge the greeting, the cowboy became perplexed. It was as if the kid was looking right through him. Glancing back over his shoulder, Autry noted who was riding just behind him in the parade. It was a big man with a white beard who was outfitted in a red suit. Smiling, Gene leaned closer to the child in an attempt to hear what he was saying. His words caused the cowboy to laughed out loud.

"Mom, look, here comes Santa Claus!"

For the first time since riding into Los Angeles, Gene Autry had been upstaged. It not only didn't bother the movie idol, it inspired him.

After the parade, the movie star went home and called his friend, composer Oakley Halderman. The two made an appointment for a songwriting session. At that meeting, Gene told the story of the parade. Using as a theme the excitement of children seeing old Saint Nick coming down the road, the duo wrote a three-verse song titled "Here Comes Santa Claus."

"Here Comes Santa Claus" reflected not only Autry's experience at the Hollywood Christmas parade but also his personal beliefs. While Gene loved the unique secular facets, traditions, and legends of Christmas in America, as the grandson of a Baptist preacher, he was also very protective of the spiritual side of the holiday. So throughout the song's first three verses, the writers subtly interjected the Christian concepts of how important it was to be a good person and how every person was loved. In the final verse of "Here Comes Santa Claus," the cowboy star's views of the significance of believing and honoring God were much more direct. There was nothing generic here. The meaning couldn't be missed.

> Peace on Earth will come to all
> If we just follow the light.
> Let's give thanks to the Lord above,
> 'Cause Santa Claus comes tonight.

"Here Comes Santa Claus" would become a huge hit. Debuting on the radio playlists in 1947, it would climb into the top ten of the pop playlists and hit the top five on the country charts. The single would also become the top children's song of the year. Over the course of the next decade, the tune would reenter the *Billboard* listings every holiday, eventually selling millions of copies and becoming the second-biggest hit in Autry's stellar recording career.

More than five decades after it was written, "Here Comes Santa Claus" remains one of the most requested Christmas standards. It is one of the few secular carols, along with "White

Christmas" and "Jingle Bells," that has been adopted by many church caroling groups. There is a genuine sweetness about this song that can be tied to the man who wrote it and first sang it. In character, personality, generosity, and love for children, the legendary Santa and the real Gene Autry were very much alike. Maybe that is why it seems that America can't have Christmas without them!

THE WASSAIL SONG

he custom of wassailing goes back at least to medieval times. A few historians have even traced parts of this ancient custom and the song to the fifth century. This makes "The Wassail Song" perhaps the very oldest carol still sung today. To put this custom and song's age into perspective, Christmas cards are about a century and a half old, and "Silent Night" was penned less than two hundred years ago, yet the Knights of the Round Table surely heard wassailers. By the 1500s the tradition was so common that Shakespeare probably had children stop at his door and sing this song. Walter Drake and Isaac Newton also must have heard the strains of the little one's hopeful voices at their gates. So the roots of "The Wassail Song" run deep, and though today it conjures up thoughts of a happy Christmas filled with good wishes and cheer, in a very real sense this song was born out of despair and great need. And underneath the happy lyrics and quaint custom is a lesson that is as important today as it was a millennium ago.

In a way, wassailing was a forerunner of caroling. Today, in certain parts of England, it is still practiced. Yet while many can sing at least one verse of the wassail carol, few actually know anything about the ancient holiday tradition that spawned the song. If carolers understood the story behind the song, they might more readily note the plight of many around them who still have few blessings to count during the Christmas season.

There are several theories as to when and why wassailing began, and while some believe the original wassailers were either single women or poor farmers, wassailing eventually grew into a tradition embracing children. In the days leading up to December 25, families who were desperately poor would decorate a large wooden bowl with colorful paint, garland, and ribbons. On Christmas Eve the families would send their children out with this bowl, usually filled with spirits, and the children would sing at the doors of the region's wealthier people. Conjuring up a Christmas card image, the custom now seems quaint, but in reality wassailing presented a picture of society that was anything but picturesque.

In old England there was a great division between the rich and the poor. The wealthy controlled not only the money but the shops, goods, and job opportunities. Essentially they were also the voice of the law in their area. The wealthy were born to privilege; by birthright they had been given the power, and there was no way to take it from them. Those without title were doomed to serve, scraping by but never getting ahead. During the winter, the children of destitute families were often hungry, cold, and poorly clothed. These waifs, as they were called, were looked at with great disdain by many members of English society.

By the sixteenth century, the Dark Ages may have been officially over, but the sun seemed to rarely shine on the poor. Scrooge in Dickens' *A Christmas Carol* had a view of children that generally fit the thoughts of that era. They were to be worked hard or even abused. The best of the lot were sometimes sold as servants to rich families. In this role they became little more than slaves. It was not a good time to be a poverty-stricken child!

Still, even though it was not usually recognized by the churches of England, in most areas Christmas was a time of celebration. During the holiday season, the poor often found a few of the lords and ladies more generous, and that is why the children went out with the wassail bowl.

The word *wassail* is derived from the Old English "Waes hael," a greeting which meant "Good health." Filling their bowl with a homemade brew, children were given directions to the homes of the leaders of the community. The singers would bring their bowl to door after door and gate after gate. In the cold, dark night, often with frigid winds blowing right through their tattered rags, they would sing at each address. Then, with eyes wide with hope, they would wait to see if their song had touched a heart.

How many doors were opened for these children? Probably only a few, but if a child received just one gift, then the effort was worth it. For a child with nothing, a copper coin was the greatest treasure in the world.

For more than a thousand years, society and wassailing changed little. Then a revolution shook the holidays. At about the same time that the English began to celebrate a Christian family Christmas, rather than the wilder and less spiritual holidays of the past, the plight of the poor was recognized and decried. Finally real light and hope came into the world of those who had lived in the shadows for so long. Churches began to reach out, government got involved, and social reforms were born. As this happened, the custom of wassailing started to become something less than it once was. No longer was a present expected when sharing a sip from the decorated bowl; now a simple "Merry Christmas" was enough.

Without the advent of caroling, "The Wassail Song" would have probably died. Yet thanks to Victorian street singers, the carol was heard in America as well as in London. And though most Americans did not understand what wassailing was, they

Here we come a wassailing
Among the leaves so green,
Here we come a wandering
So fair to be seen.

Chorus:
Love and joy come to you,
And to you your wassail too,
And God bless you and send
      you a happy New Year.
And God send you a happy
      New Year.

We are not daily beggars
That beg from door to door,
But we are neighbors' children
Whom you have seen before.

Chorus

Good Master and good
      Mistress,
As you sit by the fire,
Pray think of us poor children
Are wandering in the mire.

Chorus

We have a little purse
Made of ratching leather skin;
We want some of your small
      change
To line it well within.

Chorus

Bring us out a table,
And spread it with a cloth;
Bring us out a moldy cheese,
And some of your Christmas
      loaf.

Chorus

God bless the Master of this
      house,
Likewise the Mistress too;
And all the little children
That round the table go.

Chorus

were drawn to the old number's soft, lilting melody and haunt-ingly folksy words. And for many of those hearing it for the first time, the carol made a deep spiritual impact.

The lyrics of "The Wassail Song" present a picture of a child offering a gift of the best his family could muster. It was a humble gift, but one rich in spirit. Those who brought this bowl were not beggars but children who unfortunately had been born into poverty. They asked for little but a chance to warm by the fire and perhaps to share a bit of food or charity in exchange for the gifts of a drink and a song. What many hearing this song for the first time realized was that these chil-dren could have been the "least of these" Jesus spoke of to his disciples. So by feeding the singers, by caring for their needs, the host was able to touch and commune with the Savior.

Today "The Wassail Song" is usually sung with a final verse that was not known in ancient times. The spirit of this rather recent addition probably reflects the actual response of the children who had doors opened to them so many years ago. Back then the awed little ones probably were too surprised by the unexpected and rarely shown generosity to sing, but these words were probably on their hearts:

> *And all your kin and kinsfolk.*
> *That dwell both far and near;*
> *I wish you a merry Christmas*
> *And a happy New Year.*

IF EVERY DAY
WAS LIKE CHRISTMAS

It really is the best season of the year. The Christmas carols, trees, and lights just grab you. There's something about Christmas and being home that I just can't explain. Maybe it's being with the family and with friends, time to read and to study.

— Elvis Presley, 1966 interview,
Memphis Press Scimitar

Christmas brought out the child in Elvis Presley; it also brought out the best in him. The singer always draped his mansion and lined his driveway with blue lights. He bought Christmas trees for almost every room in the house. He made sure his family and close friends enjoyed a huge holiday dinner at his large table. After the meal, everyone would gather around the piano to sing traditional religious carols and tell stories of Christmases past. Finally Elvis would race over to the tree and eagerly pass out presents to everyone, watching closely as each of his gifts was opened. As a friend later recalled, "He really didn't care that much about getting presents, but he so enjoyed giving them."

Red West had known Presley since high school, and he, perhaps more than any other person, realized Elvis had never really fully shed the painful scars of his childhood. Presley had been a poor kid, and even though his mother did her best to make each Christmas special, most years the area under the tree was very bare. The insecurity of those days lingered even after the entertainer had the money to buy anything he wanted. Perhaps that is why he took such great pleasure in buying carloads of stuffed animals and delivering them to children's hospitals. He also loved going to car dealerships, finding someone longingly looking at a new vehicle, and buying it for them. West lost track of how many cars Elvis gave away — sometimes it was several a week — but Red never questioned the singer's sanity for being so free with his money. The grin on Presley's face was enough to assure West the entertainer got much more out of the experience than the recipient. Each Christmas, as he watched Elvis revel in the role of Graceland's Santa, West wished there could be more days just like December 25 for both the singer and the world.

Even if he had not become one of Elvis Presley's closest friends, Robert "Red" West still would have lived one of the most interesting lives of anyone who graduated from Memphis's Hume High in the 1950s. Like Presley, West grew up in the projects, a poor boy raised by a hardworking mom. Because he was a solid athlete, doors opened for him that didn't open for most students, and being a winning Golden Gloves boxer and a champion of the underdog paved the way for a close friendship with Elvis Presley. It was West who pulled the bullies off a skinny Elvis in high school. The fact that Red was willing to stand up for him when he was a nobody was something Presley never forgot.

When Elvis began to cut his teeth in the music business, he asked West to come onboard as his driver. But just when Presley's career was about to explode, West was drafted into the U.S. Marine Corps. Red therefore missed out on many of the singer's most exciting days. Still, West and Presley stayed in

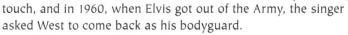

touch, and in 1960, when Elvis got out of the Army, the singer asked West to come back as his bodyguard.

While many would have been content to earn a nice paycheck by just being a part of the superstar's entourage, Red was not. When not providing security for Presley, he studied acting, initially breaking into the movies and TV as a stuntman. He first worked for Nick Adams in the hit TV series *The Rebel*, got a small part in *Spartacus*, and then began really acting in *The Wild Wild West*, *Mission Impossible*, *Battlestar Galactica*, and *Magnum P.I.* In his spare time he also composed music. Over the course of twenty years, Red penned more than 130 songs that were recorded by scores of acts, including Willie Nelson, B. J. Thomas, and Elvis. West's "Separate Ways" remains one of the most beloved hits from Presley's later years.

West understood better than most how fame had trapped Elvis Presley. He had been there in the early sixties when the star had attempted simply to walk through a Las Vegas hotel. In a venue where people paid only passive attention to stars such as Dean Martin, Cary Grant, and Frank Sinatra, tumult broke out when Presley appeared. West stepped between Elvis and the crowd as hundreds stopped what they were doing and rushed toward the young entertainer. It was then Red sadly realized his friend would never have a normal life.

Because of his immense popularity, the entertainer rarely had the chance to get out in public and enjoy the normal facets of life most people took for granted. Beginning in the early sixties, Elvis had to rent theaters to see movies or reserve amusement parks to experience the latest rides. When Presley rented the entertainment facilities and threw these parties, friends, coworkers, and associates would gather with their wives, girlfriends, and even children. While most played and had fun, Elvis often mingled with theater or park employees, enjoying the chance to visit with folks he could never meet in his own confining world.

On a late summer day in 1965, Red got a call informing him Elvis had rented a local Memphis theater and was inviting everyone to an all-night movie party. In truth, West would have rather stayed home with his wife and son, but out of a sense of loyalty he decided to make the drive over to Memphian Theater. Little did the actor-writer realize that that night would inspire a Christmas song that defined Elvis's view of the holiday.

"Halfway through the movie," Red recalled, "I got this idea for a Christmas song. I didn't want to lose it, so I jumped up and went right home to try to write." Even though this hot August night was a far cry from a snowy December eve, West found himself in a holiday mood. A part of it was the atmosphere created by the movie night. Elvis was sharing gifts and stories with his friends as if it were Christmas. This scene prompted Red to wonder, "Why can't every day be like Christmas?"

Embracing the idea that the world would be a much better place if the generous spirit of the holidays were displayed each day of the year, the writer thought of his own youth in the projects and the joy even the smallest gift would bring. He also considered the way Elvis treated the holidays. Then he looked back at the religious aspect of Christmas. It was strange how all of these memories contrasted so severely with the world he saw around him. Men were dying in Vietnam, students were protesting the war, race riots had broken out in the nation's largest cities, and the cultural gap between kids and their parents seemed too wide to breech. Popular music had become angry, and it seemed the world was brimming over with pessimism. Where was the hope that used to frame so much of the country's attitudes?

With the constant of an ideal Christmas set against the ugly picture of a world spinning out of control, Red set to work on creating a serious holiday carol. He wanted the song to echo the contrast he saw, but he wanted the lyrics to plead for people to try to treat each day with the same giving care as they did Christmas. With so many ideas spilling out of his head, West was able to pen the lyrics in less than an hour. The hauntingly beautiful tune came just as quickly.

"I recorded a pretty good demo of 'If Every Day Was Like Christmas,'" West recalled, "and then released it locally on my own label." The record hit radio stations just in time for the holidays.

Red's single got some airplay on Memphis stations but had no chance of becoming a national hit because of a lack of publicity and distribution. While West did not shop the song, Elvis heard it anyway and immediately fell in love with the new Christmas tune. A few months later RCA decided it was time to record a second Presley holiday album. When the label asked Elvis if there was anything special he wanted to put on the Christmas release, the singer sent the label West's modern carol. RCA agreed the number had hit potential.

On June 10, 1966, Presley was scheduled to come into the RCA studios and cut "If Every Day Was Like Christmas," but Elvis simply did not feel like recording that day. Rather than cancel the session, the singer called Red and asked him to work with the studio musicians, arrange and record a final version of the instrumentals and backup vocals, then lay down a lead-vocal track that could later be removed. When he felt better, the world's bestselling artist would go in by himself and lay his voice onto the otherwise finished recording.

In the studio, Presley was a perfectionist, so having West sub for him was probably a shock to many that day. RCA's lead act usually assumed complete control over his recording sessions. Elvis set the pace, played with the arrangements, decided what he wanted from his backup vocalists, and determined when he felt the product was perfect. In many cases this meant recording and re-recording a single as many as seventy times.

"You go down and cut the tracks," West remembered Elvis saying. "You sing with the band. I'll dub it in later."

Red had been staying in a hotel in Nashville, so it was an easy drive over to RCA's Studio B. As he anxiously walked into the Music Row building, he saw a number of old friends. Scotty Moore, who would be playing lead guitar, and D. J. Fontana, there with his drums, had been with Presley since the days at Sun Studios in 1954. A host of Music City's best had been hired to work with them that afternoon. Realizing the stature of the people working the session created more than a bit of doubt in Red's mind. He honestly was afraid he would not be able to measure up to the talent around him.

"I was extremely nervous," West admitted, "but these guys made me feel at ease. When I listened to what they wanted, I found it arranged just like my demo. It also felt good to have the Blackwood Brothers, Jake Hess, and Imperials at the session."

After warming up with the backup singers, Red did his best imitation of Elvis. Within an hour the tracks for "If Every Day Was Like Christmas" had been laid down.

"There had always been a special feeling around that song," West explained. "It was not a happy dancing feeling, but much more spiritual." And surrounded by some of the best gospel singers in the world, Red put a very spiritual stamp on the record that day.

As those in that June recording session realized, through his lyrics West had captured more than just the spirit of giving; he had captured the very emotions of the season. Beginning with the church bells alerting the world to the reason to be joyful, bringing in the sweet strains of a children's choir, and latching onto the dream of peace in the world, Red had painted a beautiful musical portrait of how the world was meant to be. In days filled with strife, this song longingly wished for just one day echoing the love and peace found in a true Christmas.

"I knew Elvis would do a great job recording it," Red recalled. "He was so giving; he enjoyed that facet of Christmas so much. So I felt sure the song's words and his recording would reflect his own feelings about Christmas."

Elvis was deeply touched not only by the message found in "If Every Day Was Like Christmas" but also by the sincere tone Red had used when cutting the lead vocal track. When the singer came in to overdub the number, he changed nothing. The result was one of his best singles and one of the most moving performances of his incredible career. As a music critic noted, "Like gospel music, Christmas seems to speak directly to Elvis's roots, and by listening to his performance you can tell how much he deeply believes the lyrics to this song."

"If Every Day Was Like Christmas" would become the only holiday hit Elvis Presley introduced to the world. His other seasonal singles were covers of well-known songs. Yet in this unique Christmas offering, Elvis voiced not only his own prayer but the prayer of millions when he sang:

> For if every day would be just like Christmas,
> What a wonderful world this would be.

This was a gift Red West could not give to Elvis and the singer could not give to himself, but it is a gift most of us can try to give to those around us. By living each day with the spirit we usually reserve just for Christmas, we can bring holiday cheer to others year round.

While Shepherds Watched
Their Flocks by Night

*M*ost people take it for granted that Christmas carols will be sung in church at every service between
Thanksgiving and December 25. Parishioners everywhere seem to believe that these familiar songs of the season
have been a part of worship services since the earliest days
of the Christian church. Yet in truth, the Church of England,
as well as most Protestant churches in England and America,
ignored almost all Christmas music until the middle of the
nineteenth century. So in historical terms, many denomina-
tions in general, and specifically the Anglican Church, have
only recently allowed songs other than those taken directly
from the biblical book of Psalms to be used for sanctioned services. To break down this ancient rule of worship, it would
take a spiritual poem composed by the official poet to a much
beloved English queen combined with the work of a classical
composer who once brought another member of the British
royalty to his feet.

Born in Dublin in 1652, Nahum Tate is best known today
as the author of the most famous adaptation of a Shakespeare
play. Tate had grown tired of *King Lear* and opted to rewrite
it with a happy ending. Somewhat celebrated by the common
man during Tate's life, the critics never approved, and the poet's

reworking of the English bard's famous production is now vili-
fied. So if Nahum had started and ended his literary life with the
theatrical experiment, then the world would have been denied
one of its most beautiful pieces of holiday prose, and Christmas carols might have never found their way into church services. Undaunted by the critics' condemnation of his *King Lear*,
the prolific Tate used his quill to produce a wide range of literary works. He even became so beloved throughout the British
Empire that in 1692 he succeeded Thomas Shadwell as poet
laureate of the realm, a position he held for the next twenty-
two years.

The son and grandson of clergymen, though pushed toward
the ministry, Tate jumped into literature as his calling. Over
his life he would write a host of successful musicals and many
much-appreciated short narratives. Unable to limit himself or
his work, he also composed serious prose and satirical comedy.
Yet after being assigned as his nation's official poetic voice, the
modest and good-natured writer began to focus the majority
of his attention on poetry. At the same time, he also began to
deeply examine his faith and how it affected both his actions
and the world around him.

Serious Christian poets of the era devoted their biblical
study to verses of the Old Testament. The ancient "songs" or
"poems" found in these pages were used by the church as the
basis for worship music. The only way a writer could land his
concepts of faith in a hymnal was to use one of the works
of David as inspiration. Tate understood this, and soon after
accepting the position of poet laureate, he began to focus on
updating some of the verses he found in his own Bible.

In 1696, the poet developed a metrical version of the book
of Psalms. His goal had been not to change any of the original
meanings of the verses but to update them in a way that would
make them easier to use in modern song worship. If he had just
stopped there, he would have created something worthwhile

for his church but probably not made history. Tate, who had proven his fearlessness when he dared to rework Shakespeare, opted to march beyond Psalms. In fact he didn't stop exploring until he had gotten to the New Testament and the events surrounding the birth of Jesus.

For reasons even he could not fully explain, Tate found himself particularly drawn to Luke 2:8–14. He felt this passage offered real understanding of the way even common people could respond to God's call and accomplish wonderful things. The poet must have also sensed a commonality to these verses and many of those found in Psalms. The theme of the shepherd and the sheep was one that was echoed throughout the Old Testament. Yet more than the obvious connection between old and new, the fact that God had invited these humble field workers to share the joy of Christ's birth must have overwhelmed Tate. In his mind, this had to be the most incredible birthday-party invitation ever issued. Yet there was more to the story than just the revelation; it was that these men accepted God's challenge and went to the stable. Though they had every reason not to, they gave up everything to follow the Lord's lead. These facts made this small bit of Scripture one of the most powerful passages Tate had ever read.

Though he knew it violated every rule of worship, the poet began to rework that passage in Luke. He was determined to create a new song, all the while knowing the Church of England would have no part of it when he finished. So like the shepherds were inspired to make a long trip based only on faith, Tate continued to work on his song until he had concluded his new carol. Some time later, after finishing his edits to the book of Psalms, he dropped his "While Shepherds Watched Their Flocks by Night" into his final manuscript and passed it on to the Anglican priests in charge of publishing new hymnals. As the clergymen read his original addition, they could not have been more shocked if Moses had reappeared, come down from

Whilst shepherds watched
their flocks by night,
All seated on the ground,
The angel of the Lord came
down,
And glory shone around,
And glory shone around.
Fear not, said he, for mighty
dread
Had seized their troubled
mind.
Glad tidings of great joy I
bring
To you and all mankind
To you and all mankind.
To you, in David's town, this
day
Is born of David's line
A Savior, which is Christ the
Lord,
And this shall be the sign,
And this shall be the sign.
The heavenly Babe you there
shall find
To human view displayed,
All meanly wrapped in swad-
dling bands,
And in a manger laid,
And in a manger laid.
Thus spake the Seraph, and
forthwith
Appeared a heavenly throng
Of Angels praising God and
thus,
Addressed their joyful song,
Addressed their joyful song.
All glory be to God on high,
And to the earth be peace;
Good will henceforth from
heaven to earth
Begin and never cease,
Begin and never cease!

the mount a second time, and announced a revision to the Ten Commandments. Some had to have said, "Surely he knows better than to create a song from anywhere but Psalms!"

The biblical scholars might have been surprised by Tate's New Testament poem, but they didn't immediately dismiss it. In fact, some of them found the poet's intense study of the Scripture in "While Shepherds Watched Their Flocks by Night" interesting. Some admired the fact that, unlike many amateur carol composers of the era, who had committed such fallacies as having the wise men and shepherds arrive at the same time, Tate took no liberties with the Scripture. He invented nothing new and added no imagery that any reader of the Bible could not find on his or her own. Several pointed out that the writer's dedicated adherence to the original story might be useful in holiday worship. It could be used as a teaching tool, some argued. Yet even as good as it was, was "While Shepherds Watched Their Flocks by Night" worth breaking a long-held church tradition?

The dilemma was not resolved quickly. If the church leaders allowed Tate's original work to pass muster, then they were opening the door for other writers to create original hymns not based on the Psalms. Ultimately, most of the leaders of the time admitted they liked Tate's new poem and genuinely felt it was true to the biblical text, but they felt it was simply not inspired by the parts of the Bible meant for singing. So they reasoned it should not be included when his reworking of the Psalms of David was published and given to church congregations. As it turned out, there was another factor at play that would help create a rather revolutionary decision.

Though they had determined that Tate's new song was not in accordance with church history, the leaders of the Anglican Church also realized Tate was the nation's poet laureate. As such, he had the power of royalty behind him. So rather than anger Queen Anne, the church allowed "While Shepherds

Watched Their Flocks by Night" to be included with the new versions of the Psalms. Thus, thanks in large part to his friends in high places, Tate's work would become the first Christmas-inspired song to appear in an Anglican hymnal.

Tate did not compose any music for his new hymn, so initially the words were sung to a wide variety of different tunes. Ultimately, it would be a composer who created one of history's most powerful Christmas anthems, "The Hallelujah Chorus," that would write the perfect melody for "While Shepherds Watched Their Flocks by Night." Yet this marriage of verse and song would occur after Tate had passed away. So when Nahum heard his poem used in worship services, it sounded much different than it does today.

Initially, many congregations sang "While Shepherds Watched" to "Winchester Old." This was an old British folk tune dating back to the 1500s. Yet as solid as that union was, it would be a selection from George Handel's huge body of work that would best lend itself to the Anglican Church's first accepted Christmas carol.

In 1728, a decade after Tate had died, Handel wrote the opera *Siroe, King of Persia*. A tune from *Siroe* quickly became one of the best-known melodies in Britain. Astute church musicians soon discovered that this tune from the Handel opera perfectly matched the poetic meter of "While Shepherds Watched Their Flocks by Night." So while Tate's poem has been sung to scores of different melodies, including the tune of "It Came upon a Midnight Clear," it is Handel's contribution to this work that remains the most popular, giving the famous composer a role in two Christmas works that most closely adhere to biblical text.

When viewed in today's light there would seem to be nothing earth-shattering about "While Shepherds Watched." It is a beautiful lyrical treatment of the passage from Luke, but it hardly seems a candidate to start a revolution. Yet these lyrics launched a much-needed movement in the Anglican Church that dramatically enhanced worship for both clergy and laity. As the first original Christmas hymn, it set the foundation for a church celebration of Jesus' birth. Yet even though it broke new ground and proved instantly popular with congregations on both sides of the Atlantic, church leaders remained unconvinced that anyone but Tate could create a Christmas hymn worthy of including in worship services. It was to be another eighty years before another new holiday work, "Angels from the Realms of Glory," followed "While Shepherds Watched Their Flocks by Night" and found acceptance in official church psalters, what most know today as hymnals. It would be another seven decades before the musical Christmas revolution was complete and Protestant churches in England and America really warmed up to singing carols in houses of worship.

IT WASN'T HIS CHILD

kip Ewing had been trying to carve out a niche in country music since moving to Nashville in 1984 at the age of twenty. Though a talented musician, a solid vocalist, and an imaginative songwriter, for three years he found himself one of hundreds struggling to find a small piece of Music City's spotlight. In 1987, MCA signed Ewing to a record deal, and a year later he landed two top-ten singles. Even though he was earning radio spins and had other artists recording his tunes, he was a long way from being a headlining act. So for every moment of success he had experienced since setting out on his own, he had faced a similar number of disappointments.

Just before Christmas, Skip finished up his appearances for 1988. Armed with the song "Burnin' a Hole in My Heart," which was steadily climbing the charts, he climbed into his car and headed west. He was going home, and that meant a couple of thousand miles of open road before pulling into his mother's California driveway.

In so many ways this was the best holiday season he had ever known. He was beginning to live his dreams, and in his family's eyes, he had become a star. Yet no matter how perfect this Christmas seemed, when held up against the light of an imperfect world, a bit of depression still crowded into Ewing's mind, spilling over into his heart. All the way home, he was praying for a Christmas miracle. Yet as soon as he walked in the front door, he knew his prayers had not been answered.

"My mother and father were divorced," Skip explained, "and quite frankly, my childhood was very difficult for a number of reasons. I was still hopeful that relationships could be good among the wider circle of my family. I got out there and realized that things were probably not going to ever change, and it was quite frustrating."

Even though his hope for family healing was quickly dashed, Ewing nevertheless was glad to be home. The familiar decorations had been hung, presents were stacked under the tree, and his mother had made sure his favorite foods were waiting for him. Though he was surrounded by all this holiday magic, dealing with the disappointment of not having the perfect family still lingered in his thoughts. That evening that disappointment began to bloom into a song concept.

"I always try to remember to be of a beginner's mind," Skip explained. "In that way I can learn and relearn what I have already learned. So I am always evolving and being more sensitive to the needs of other people and what they are dealing with at that moment. At that time it was a heightened awareness of the relationships of family that was dominating my thoughts."

With family on his mind, the writer began to consider the first family of Christmas. He began to think of Joseph and Mary, as well as all of those around them in the days before the birth of Christ.

"As I was processing things about Christmas," Ewing recalled, "it dawned on me that at the time that Mary and Joseph were actually together, a betrothal was more important or more binding than the marriage. The marriage was the ceremony, but the betrothal was the commitment. I began to think about what Joseph must have thought when he found out that his wife was having this child. I was thinking about this man and how he must have been filled with faith and great trust for his wife. He was hugely instrumental in keeping something special together. The more I explored that in my mind, the more I thought how much I would have respected him for the way he handled that situation."

Skip is a very deep thinker, a man who carefully studies people and their various reactions to the trials of life. When he first goes into writing mode, he carefully analyzes his source of inspiration on several different levels. On this holiday eve, as he examined one participant in the Christmas story, his mind began to consider what Joseph's song would sound like.

"If he was gentle in his understanding, compassionate, and thoughtful," Ewing explained, "I began to question what that would feel like musically. Considering that, I came up with this guitar movement that just sort of falls under your fingers. It was not an easy thing to play, but once I was moving with it, it felt good to me. As I listened to it, I thought there was goodness in it."

With the first musical riffs in place and his song's subject known, the writer then began to imagine how the story of Joseph and his relationship with his son needed to be laid out. As if working with the most fragile piece of antique glass, Skip examined the story from every angle. His exhaustive inspection reflected the light of inspired direction.

"I thought, wow, it is not actually Joseph's child, but at the same time, it is bigger than if he had been his own child. Jesus would have had this man as a role model. Jesus would see love and acceptance through Joseph. And even though Jesus was as spiritual as he was, he still must have grown and been given such wonderful gifts from both his earthly parents."

Deciding he wanted his song to deal with fatherhood, Ewing penned his first verse about a man raising a son that was not his own. He did this without giving away the fact that the boy was actually the Son of God.

"The first part I wrote," Skip explained, "I wanted it not to be clear that it was Jesus. There have been many people who have cared for and loved children who were not their own, not of their blood. And there was no difference in the way they loved these children. I wanted the first verse to explain that unconditional love is unconditional love no matter who is involved. That is one of the greatest gifts we can give to anyone.

"So I wrote the first part to feel as though it could have been an adopted son. Then, in the second verse, you realize it is Jesus. The song then moves to a different relationship of father and son."

The chorus could be applied to either father-son relationship, but it also served another purpose. While the second verse was a Christmas proclamation of the divinity of Christ, Ewing felt a real need to put the spotlight back on the love, acceptance, and compassion Joseph had for both Jesus and Mary. So he ended his musical story by going back to its beginning.

"I wanted to have the opening verse be a window that opens twice," the writer revealed. "It reiterates the initial facts, and your understanding is increased by hearing the message of what Joseph did twice."

Ewing's diligent effort was due to his drive to create something worthy of the strength he saw in this biblical story. Thus he refused to compromise a single word, carefully crafting every phrase and verse. Nothing was overlooked, which resulted in a lyric line that was both poetic and insightful. Examining all that Joseph had taught Jesus, even his passing along the skills of carpentry, brought Christ's life alive in a new way and even foreshadowed the price he paid on the cross.

"To me," Skip explained, "lines like 'He grew up with his hands in wood and he died with his hands in wood' helped show that these were real people. I think that is also an important message. Joseph was a man who gave of himself in a great way. He was heroic of heart. Something I hope we all would work toward being."

As night became early morning, the song was close to being completed. But as profound as its message was, the writer did not feel he had yet done the story justice.

"I didn't want to force something," Ewing continued. "I don't like something to be contrived. I like for the heart of something to be always there and for it to be something that is offered and not pushed at a listener. Because for me, this way of looking at Joseph and Jesus was a discovery too. I was trying to hold it gently and say, 'How can I grow at the same time I am writing this song?'"

Skip's mother's family Christmas was held the next day at an aunt's home. As some of his great uncles and his grandmother had once been vaudeville entertainers, the country musician took his guitar along to provide music for some of the songs they liked to sing each year. Yet all through the dinner, and the fun and fellowship of that afternoon, Ewing's mind kept returning to his unfinished song. He felt driven to write, but he didn't want to be rude and leave the scores of people of all ages who had come together on this special day.

Finally, unable to think of anything but his unfinished project, he asked his aunt if there was a place he could go and write. She pointed him toward the one bedroom that was empty. Closing the door, Ewing knelt down on the floor and tried to concentrate. But with children banging on a piano, with laughter echoing from seemingly every corner, with a dozen muffled conversations coming through the walls at the same time, it was almost impossible.

"I sat kneeling on the far side of the room with my hands pressing on my ears so I couldn't hear anything but what was inside my head. I was right on the edge of finding what I needed, but it was almost too frustrating. I worked on it and worked on it, and finally I thought I had it."

After placing the finishing touches on the new composition, the young man returned to the party. When his grandmother found out what he had been doing in the bedroom, she asked him to debut it for the family. It would be the first time Skip would get to sing "It Wasn't His Child" all the way through. As he played the new song, the house became quiet for the first time that day. When he finished the final chord, the looks on his family's faces told him he had produced something very special.

After the holidays, Ewing went into the studio and cut a demo of the new Christmas song. Before he could place it on one of his own albums, Sawyer Brown recorded "It Wasn't His Child." The country group's version would become a holiday hit the next Christmas. Trisha Yearwood then followed that with her own version, then a host of others from every musical genre put their spin on Ewing's holiday number. Reba McEntire used it on her television series, and Tug McGraw sang it at the Nobel Prize ceremony, where it left an audience awestruck. Within a decade, "It Wasn't His Child" was elevated to classic status. "Rudolph the Red-Nosed Reindeer" is the only other number first introduced in country music that has become such a universally accepted holiday carol.

When he speaks of his musical goals, Ewing's faith and character are revealed. "I want to put things out there that have a lot of love, light, and positivity. I believe in reaching and touching someone. The listener trusts me enough to let me into their hearts and minds. If they trust me that much, I am not going to take advantage of that trust. I am going to respect that and give them something worthy of that trust."

With his magnificent Christmas offering "It Wasn't His Child," Ewing has touched millions of people. He has shed new light on the most powerful story ever told. He has, in a very real sense, put the holiday spotlight on someone who has usually been overlooked. Skip also brought a unique humanity and dimension to a story that often is viewed in very static form. By the way he so carefully crafted "It Wasn't His Child," he gave the world a song that truly reflects God's love for his people. It accomplishes this not only through its dynamic words and beautiful music but through the fact that this carol really doesn't end.

"At the end of 'It Wasn't His Child,'" Ewing divulged, "when it says, 'He was God's child,' I used an unresolved chord. Because to me the story is still alive. There is no ending to it. In fact, for all of us it is a never-ending pursuit."

This never-ending pursuit began that first Christmas, was born with a child, and lives on today for all of God's children. It is what Jesus brought to earth, what God revealed in him, and what Joseph stood for as both a husband and a father.

21

PRETTY PAPER

hristmas songs that evoke social consciousness are usually not very popular. Carols that attempt to shed light on the plight of the poor or oppressed, or that try to point out the futility of war or prejudice, are often pushed aside or quickly dismissed as being too depressing for the vibrant holiday season. So the few seasonal offerings that managed to thrive while combining stories of holiday joy with the stark realities of poverty and despair are often well-written works whose message of need is somehow wrapped in a holiday package of music that appears bright and beautiful. An example of this type of social message song can been found in the still-popular work by Henry Wadsworth Longfellow "I Heard the Bells on Christmas Day" and in the famous Charles Dickens' story *A Christmas Carol*. More than one hundred years after these two famous works became holiday traditions, another holiday social classic was written by a modern-day country poet named Willie Nelson.

Nelson's slow rise from poverty to superstardom is the stuff of American legend and laid the background for many of his most popular songs. Like his good friend Roger Miller, Willie grew up on the outside looking in. Poor, pushed aside, and often misunderstood, the Abbott, Texas, native kicked around dance halls and small town radio stations before arriving in Houston in the fifties. Though a talented songwriter, the small man with the trembling voice couldn't find much success in the oil center of the Gulf Coast. He made car payments and fed his family by teaching guitar and selling rights to some of his songs. Always desperate for cash, Willie traded future royalties to such classics as "Born to Lose" and "Family Bible" for as little as fifty dollars. When the bad times in Texas grew even worse, the young man moved to Nashville.

In the early sixties, Music City was alive with talent. The Tennessee city was home to dozens of the greatest tunesmiths in the world, and it seemed on every street corner there was another wannabe songwriter trying to pitch a guitar case full of new melodies. At first Nelson had problems finding anyone to record one of his pieces. He got by on the charity of performers who were more impressed with his determination and gentle manners than his talent. Perseverance and months of eating catsup sandwiches finally won out when Faron Young's recording of Willie's "Hello Walls" began to pay for some meals, and Patsy Cline's cut of Nelson's "Crazy" took the young man off the streets for good.

After so many years of barely scraping by, no matter how large his bank account grew, Willie never forgot what it was like to be hungry, cold, and forgotten at Christmas. In the years before becoming "an overnight success," Nelson had grown to accept that Santa simply didn't stop at his house. So even after he had made his mark in Music City, the Texas songwriter remembered that there were scores of men and women living on the streets who were hanging on the edge between life and death. And Willie, who had also traveled a great deal, knew that America was full of people who had somehow gotten lost, been pushed out of society, and were now wandering along endless roads with no home, no family, and no hope. Nelson's heart never stopped hurting for these unfortunate souls either.

While many of Nelson's personal sins have been well documented over the years, what has often been forgotten is his charity. Quietly, as he began to make a little money, Willie sought out the world's underdogs and stuck a few dollars in their pockets. While other stars quickly moved through crowds and rushed into the safety of guarded doors, Nelson often sat down on a curb with the homeless to listen to their stories and see if there was any way he could help. His actions assured all those around him that he had not forgotten where he had once been and had not lost the feelings that came with living on the outside looking in.

When Nelson wrote the song "Pretty Paper," he had to be thinking of his own years spent in poverty. It was still the early sixties, and the singer-songwriter had not been on the charts enough even to feel secure about his own career and future. Yet Nelson, whose long list of finely crafted tunes now stands as a testament to his understanding of people and life, probably didn't immediately realize the eventual impact of his seemingly autobiographical holiday effort. "Pretty Paper" was not only a beautiful country ballad about both the happy and sad sides of the Christmas season, but its secondary story of a poor man looking into the world of holiday dreams from the outside was a moving treatment of the social ills that are still a part of society today. And when that poor suffering man cries as others celebrate the most joyous time of the year, it shows just how blind most Americans are to the pain and hopelessness all around them.

Texas's Roy Orbison would first record "Pretty Paper" in 1963. Orbison's emotional voice was a perfect fit for Nelson's tear-jerking ode to a man who seems to have lost everything he holds dear. Orbison's final pleading cut was stirring, pained, and inspired.

Though many during the sixties would fail to understand the song's real message, and few would notice the plight of the poor or the homeless even after listening to its tormented, almost-hidden storyline, along with "Blue Christmas," "Rockin' around the Christmas Tree," and "Jingle Bell Rock," "Pretty Paper" would earn a spot as one of the rock era's biggest holiday hits. It would also become one of the few country-music-inspired holiday songs to make a lasting impact on American music.

Orbison's version of Nelson's "Pretty Paper" would prove to be so popular that a host of artists would rush out to cover it. Even Willie himself would cut a recording of the tune. Yet though it became an annual favorite on country and rock stations, it would take almost three decades for the song's weighty message to fully emerge from under the song's hauntingly beautiful melody and finely crafted lyrics. In the late eighties, when "Pretty Paper" was played, disc jockeys, performers, and even preachers began to note the nation's many homeless and poor people. There were millions, some of them children, who couldn't help but see Christmas all around them but never had the spirit of the season touch their lives. During these tough times, Willie's subtle message wrapped into a beautifully crafted package was finally hitting home.

While there is no mention of the birth or life of Jesus in Willie Nelson's Christmas classic, it presents a stark picture of the kind of person whom the Lord sought out and touched during his time on earth. Nelson's haunting lyrics therefore draw a vivid portrait of one of "the least of these." And in the song "Pretty Paper," the response of those who walk by this poor person is much the same as those who lived during Jesus' time, as well as those who live today—they ignore him.

For those who feel left out of the holiday spirit, Christmas is the loneliest time of the year. When so many are so happy and so caught up in buying and giving, those who will not be with family, will not receive a gift or a card, and will be forgotten or ignored even as choirs stroll by them singing carols, will shed the tears that Nelson described in "Pretty Paper." Perhaps that is why Christmas carols need to remind us not only to celebrate the birth of the Savior but also to live and give the way the Lord taught, to see the wrongs and set them right, and to do our part to bring joy, happiness, and peace to those living on the outside looking in. This is the subtle message found when all the pretty paper is unwrapped.

22

AVE MARIA

wo of the most creative men of the classical era combined to complete the work on one of the most haunting songs sung at Christmas. Vienna's great composer
Franz Schubert created the haunting melody and arrangement
for "Ave Maria," while the carol's soaring lyrics flowed from
the pen of the famed Scottish writer Sir Walter Scott. Yet while
these two distinguished men are usually given exclusive credit
for the wonderful holiday offering, and they no doubt carved
much of their faith into the final product, the song has roots
that go back more than a thousand years before either Schubert
or Scott was born.

Many of the lyrics now attributed to Scott were actually
a part of the Marian prayer known as the "Hail Mary." Gre-
gorian monks performed this song for centuries before it was
ever sung outside the church. A musical prayer always sung in
Latin, when translated into English "Hail Mary" reads, "Hail
Mary, full of grace, the Lord is with thee. Blessed art thou
amongst women and blessed is the fruit of thy womb, Jesus.
Holy Mary, Mother of God, pray for us sinners, now, and at the
hour of our death. Amen."

A majority of the original prayer comes from the Gospel of
Luke and joins together the words of the angel Gabriel found in
the first chapter of Luke, verse twenty-eight, with Elizabeth's
greeting to Mary found in the forty-second verse of the same

chapter. Early church records indicate the prayer and song probably date back to the fourth or fifth century and were first used in worship services in either Antioch or Alexandria.

The chanted prayer remained much the same for over a thousand years. Then an additional verse was added. This stanza was not based on any specific biblical text but spoke of Mary's importance in becoming a part of God's plan of salvation and her role in bringing the Lord's word to life. This adapted version of "Hail Mary" dates back to at least 1568, when it was spoken by Pope St. Pius V.

Not to be outdone by church scribes, Shakespeare created a version as well. The great English bard naturally wrote his "Ave Maria" in English.

> Ave Maria! Maiden mild!
> O listen to a maiden's prayer!
> For thou canst hear amid the wild
> (For thou canst hear though from the wild)
> Tis thou, tis thou canst save amid despair.
> We slumber safely 'til the morrow,
> (Safe may we sleep beneath thy care,)
> Tho' we, by men, outcast, reviled;
> (Tho' banish'd, outcast, and reviled;)
> Maiden! hear a maiden's prayer;
> Mother, hear a suppliant child!
> Ave Maria!

Like the official church prayers, Shakespeare emphasized the humble grace of Jesus' mother. Like the church, he also put Mary above all other women in history. As the English writer had penned odes about some of history's most important female players, his elevation of the mother of Christ probably revealed a great deal about his own faith.

Sir Walter Scott was the next major personality to put his stamp on the ancient church prayer. Born in Edinburgh, Scotland,

Latin:
Ave Maria Gratia plena
Maria Gratia plena
Maria Gratia plena
Ave, ave dominus
Dominus tecum
Benedicta tu in mulieribus
Et benedictus
Et benedictus fructus ventris
Ventris tui Jesus

Ave Maria
Ave Maria Mater dei
Ora pro nobis pecatoribus
Ora, ora pro nobis
Ora ora pro nobis pecatoribus
Nunc et in hora mortis
In hora mortis, mortis nostrae
In hora mortis nostrae
Ave Maria!

English:
Ave Maria! Ave Maria! Maiden mild!
Listen to a maiden's prayer!
Thou canst hear though from the wild,
Thou canst save amid despair.
Safe may we sleep beneath thy care,
Though banish'd, outcast and reviled —
Maiden! hear a maiden's prayer;
Mother, hear a suppliant child!
Ave Maria!

Ave Maria! undefiled!
The flinty couch we now must share
Shall seem this down of eider piled,
If thy protection hover there.
The murky cavern's heavy air
Shall breathe of balm if thou hast smiled;
Then, Maiden! hear a maiden's prayer;
Mother, list a suppliant child!
Ave Maria!

Ave Maria! stainless styled!
Foul demons of the earth and air,
From this their wonted haunt exiled,
Shall flee before thy presence fair.
We bow us to our lot of care,
Beneath thy guidance reconciled;
Hear for a maid a maiden's prayer,
And for a father hear a child!
Ave Maria!

in 1771, Scott was still a young man when he emerged as the most popular author of the era of human enlightenment. The writer was one of the first to weave historical stories in such a way as to have common people interacting with those who impacted world history. A strong believer in reaching out to the poor with charity and kindness, he was the first novelist to portray peasant characters as three-dimensional people with real problems. In Scott's work, the lower class was treated with the same respect and dignity as the nation's rulers.

Scott reflected the same kindness in real life as he did in his work. He was known for his generosity. He always made an effort to include the common people in his personal celebrations and triumphs. His door was open to all his neighbors, no matter their class, and he often reached out to the needy wherever he traveled. In fact, it could be said that he lived his entire life by the famous line he wrote in *Marmion*, "Oh, what a tangled web we weave, when first we practice to deceive!" Scott simply did not deceive anyone in life or in his writings. Thus when he placed his version of "Ave Maria" in his famous *The Lady of the Lake*, he did so because of the importance he placed on Mary's spot in history. Happy that he could work a bit of his own faith into the pages of one of his bestsellers, little did Scott know his book would soon inspire another artist living on the other side of Europe to add the final dimension needed to make "Ave Maria" a holiday classic.

In 1825, twenty-eight-year-old Franz Schubert read *The Lady of the Lake* and was overwhelmed. Schubert was the son of a schoolteacher and, as a child, studied piano, violin, organ, singing, and harmony. At the age of twenty-four the composer had already produced piano pieces, string quartets, his first symphony, and a three-act opera. Over the next few years, the volume of his classical work was overshadowed only by the quality of his music. Already one of Europe's most-beloved musical talents, the composer continued to add depth and emotion to his work. Interjecting so much of his own beliefs into his music set him apart from almost all of the other composers of his day. While scores of his pieces are now regarded as classics, he personally felt he peaked when he was inspired to write melodies for a Sir Walter Scott poem. Unable to read English, the composer was introduced to *The Lady of the Lake* through Adam Storck's German translation.

Seized by the power he felt in the section that concluded with the prayer "Ave Maria," Schubert developed a simple but soaring melody to accompany the prose. The composer felt the prayer was so personal that his musical arrangement was not for a full orchestra but only for voice and piano. Just playing and singing the song by himself seemed to bring him closer to God. Schubert called his piece "Ellens dritter Gesang" ("Ellen's Third Song"). The title was taken from the Scott story in which one of the lead characters, Ellen Douglas, is in hiding and prays to the Virgin Mary.

Overwhelmed by what he viewed as his best work, Schubert wrote his father, "My new songs from Scott's *Lady of the Lake* especially had much success. They also wondered greatly at my piety, which I expressed in a hymn to the Holy Virgin and which, it appears, grips every soul and turns it to devotion."

Sadly, Schubert did not get to enjoy his success or fully come to understand the power of his work. Less than three years after completing what he viewed as his greatest gift to the world, the composer died at the age of thirty-one. Yet "Ave Maria" didn't just survive; its popularity grew beyond that of any of the man's other works and well beyond the popularity of Scott's large library of timeless literary classics.

There has long been a special spotlight placed on Mary in the Catholic Church that does not exist in other Christian circles. So for many who come from a Protestant background, the way the lyrics of "Ave Maria" present the mother of Jesus might seem a bit foreign. Yet what all Christian faiths do recognize is the dynamic place this humble woman holds in fulfilling God's plan for mankind. Without Mary's acceptance of God's will, Scott and Schubert would not have been inspired to give the world "Ave Maria." In fact, there would not have been a Christmas at all. So Mary, no doubt, deserves to be remembered and honored by one of the season's most beautiful carols as she reminds each of us of the incredible gift God gives us in Jesus.

23

CHRISTMAS IN THE COUNTRY

or the past generation, Bill Gaither has been the best-
known Christian songwriter on the globe. His love
of gospel music and his spirit of Christian outreach
have exposed countless thousands to the inspiration of gospel
music. His Homecoming concert series has brought together
on one stage some of the greatest legends in the Christian
music world and allowed them to share with millions of fans
some of the most moving songs ever written. Yet though these
programs have now sold out in huge metropolises all around
the world and though Gaither is constantly in demand from
London to Los Angeles, the lure of big city lights doesn't hold
his attention for long. After each tour Bill always comes home
to a very rural section of Indiana.

Gaither grew up on a farm outside of Anderson. His family
roots are dug deeply in the midwestern soil. Even as he learned
to play the piano, he also was taught how to use his hands to
till the earth. As a teen he sweated out long summer afternoons
working in hay fields and cleaning out barns, and bundled up
during the cold short days of winter shoveling snow and milk-
ing cows. Though he didn't always look forward to the hard
work, he understood its value, as well as the importance of the
responsibilities his family had entrusted to him.

Even after he left home to go to college, even after he got a
job teaching high school, and even after he married Gloria, each

holiday season Gaither continued to come back to the family farm. To the songwriter, this was where Christmas really came alive. Every time he walked in the home's front door, again seeing the corner where the family Christmas tree always stood, the familiar decorations that had been used and reused for years, the kitchen table filled with homemade candy and pies, and the brightly wrapped gifts stacked all around the evergreen, scores of old memories flooded his mind. It was a moment like none other, an instant when past and present melded into a single emotional thread defined by hope, love, and joy. As time passed and the family gained some members and lost others, Gaither continued to experience this rush with each new visit during every holiday season. As he continued to build on that mountain of memories, the spirit and real meaning of Christmas grew stronger and clearer.

Bill and Gloria celebrated more than three decades of creating timeless gospel music before turning their attention to their favorite time of the year. Though the duo had penned scores of the most celebrated Christian songs ever written, they had never concentrated their talents on Christmas music. Yet on the final Christmas Eve of the last century, as the two came back together with family in the familiar old farmhouse and as the love and spirit surrounded them once more, they began to consider the ramifications of the greatest event ever to happen in the history of the planet.

It is obvious from songs such as "He Touched Me" and "The King Is Coming" that the Gaithers had long thought of the life of Christ as the world's greatest story. It was their inspiration in every bit of music they created. Now surrounded by the memories of their own rural Christmases, the couple began to examine in a very new light the events that happened in a Bethlehem stable.

"We were home for the holidays," Bill explained as he thought of the reason he and his wife felt moved to create a holiday carol. "It was a rural setting, life here was slower than it normally was for us, and we got the chance to again get very close to God through nature."

For Gaither, being at the family's country home always brought him closer to his maker. Thus it was not surprising he felt a fresh desire to create an autobiographical song that captured the spiritual holidays he had experienced and so loved. While it would be rural memories that set the foundation for the song, it would be a writing session with a former country singer where the idea began to take shape.

Woody Wright had once been part of an up and coming music trio called Matthews, Wright, and King. The group had toured the nation for several years, creating a new fan base while they opened for the hottest acts in Nashville. Just when it seemed their music was about to take off, the band broke up. The Tennessee-born Wright was suddenly forced to go back to his rural roots and reevaluate his goals. If it hadn't been for his strong faith and a work ethic taught by country chores, he probably would have given up on the music business. Yet he kept writing and kept plugging away. Eventually his work was noticed by Gaither, and the two became friends. Through Bill's urging, Woody moved to Christian music. Soon he found himself writing songs with the Gaithers.

Sensing that telling the story of what his own Christmases were really like would take the perspective of a man who had spent some time in country music, Bill set up an appointment with Woody. Bill and Woody both learned teamwork in their youth. To get farm chores finished, it took everyone doing their part. So working as a team on a writing project was second nature to both of them. They each believed that by coming together and pooling their talents the final product would be much better. After Bill explained the concept he wanted, Wright and Gaither combined on a melody that was part Stamps-Baxter gospel tune and part Bob Wills swing. Satisfied they had created a suitable framework for the story, Gaither took the music to his wife.

"Gloria knew my experiences as well as I did," Bill explained. "So when she wrote the lyrics, it was exactly what I pictured as we created the music. Gloria wrote a song that seemed initially secular in nature, but then the lyrics bridged the gap to the original Christmas story."

The new Gaither song would debut at a Homecoming Christmas concert during the last part of the first year of the twenty-first century. Immediately during rehearsals, the Homecoming singers fell in love with the new holiday offering. Though these men and women came from all over the country and had experienced scores of different holiday customs and traditions, the song's message hit home to each of them in a very special way. The legends who first gave their voices to the new work realized that "Christmas in the Country" had accomplished what few holiday songs could; it was universal in message and appeal.

Like a Currier and Ives painting or the set of the movie *Holiday Inn*, Gloria's lyrics embraced all the rich fabric found in a rural Christmas. In the first two verses and chorus, she carefully revealed the simple things found in a country holiday, such as the gathering of the family, church groups singing carols, the sense of warmth, the gentleness of a loved one's touch, and the memories of holidays so long ago. Like a Norman Rockwell illustration, she also captured the smell of homemade candy, the sights of colorful bubble lights, and the secret whispers of children as they studied the presents under the lavishly decorated handcut evergreen. So at this point, those who initially heard the carol when it made its debut, probably considered "Christmas in the Country" as little more than a beautiful but secular holiday song. They didn't yet grasp the full meaning found in the subtle line "the old love story." For the moment it seemed like these four words were simply saluting the coming together of generations of family members. It was in the third verse that the real message of "Christmas in the Country" is revealed.

The final act of this four-minute musical play begins when the father pulls out a well-worn Bible. Suddenly from the oldest grandparent to the youngest child, a transformation takes place. Each of the guests grows quiet, while they turn their attention to the family patriarch. With a hushed but firm voice, filled with deep reverence and etched in emotion, the man begins to read the words found in the second chapter of Luke. As he does, the song's inspired lyrics spill out the story of how God loved his people enough to send his Son to die for all of their sins. This is, the last stanza explains, the real "simple old love story."

"I am a farm kid," Bill proudly stated as he finished talking about his carol. "I remember how excited I was on Christmas Eves as I did my chores. During that time of the year in Indiana, it was often dark by four in the afternoon. I had to get the cows in, make sure the animals were bedded down, and then clean up for our Christmas Eve. Each year, something wonderful and magical happened. With her lyrics Gloria perfectly captured the family Christmas I so deeply loved."

"Christmas in the Country" has become one of the few Southern gospel songs to have made an impact on the holiday season. In just five years, the carol has found an audience well beyond gospel music. Naturally the song has been picked up by country music artists, but it has also taken root in church celebrations across America. Because of its unique mix of postcard Christmas imagery coupled with its infectious melody, the carol has even found a place in the secular music scene. Yet the inspiration that continues to make this new carol more popular each holiday season is the ingenious way it reshapes and emphasizes the reason people come together each December 25. Bill, Gloria, and Woody knew the holidays were about family because they began with a family. The first Christmas was also a "Christmas in the Country." Those who initially arrived to witness the occasion were shepherds, and surrounding the baby were the same creatures who two thousand years later can still be found in barns. So even while this new song created a new spin to the old love story, it really has always been "Christmas in the Country."

COME AND SEE WHAT'S
HAPPENING IN THE BARN

*I*t is indeed strange to conceive of anything very monumental happening in a barn. Yet for reasons known only in heaven, it was ordained for Jesus to draw his first earthly breath surrounded by curious animals rather than worshiping masses. At first glance, this hardly appeared to be a royal birth and was not one that seemed worth recording at that moment, much less one that the world still celebrates two thousand years later. Yet in spite of this humble setting, a few folks did notice.

The community where Jesus was born was hardly a teaming metropolis. It was a tiny rural village that offered little in the way of opportunity or culture. So it is not surprising that there were no rooms available when Joseph and Mary arrived in Bethlehem. Due to a Roman census, when law decreed that people had to return to their ancestral homes to be counted, a great many people were traveling the roads of Judea. Salesmen and herders had been joined by numerous families, among them Joseph and Mary. So naturally the few rooms in the local inns had been taken long before the newlyweds arrived in the town.

Sensing that camping out under the stars would not be a good thing for the pregnant woman, it was probably the innkeeper who suggested checking out a local stable. At least the barn would offer a bit of coverage from the cool nights or the occasional rains. With no other options, the couple prayed that at least they might find a warm spot in one of the stalls.

After the long trip riding a burro across the roads of Judea, Mary must have been exhausted. Knowing that now she had to bed down with the area's animals had to have been disappointing to the young woman. Yet here she was, probably surrounded by horses and donkeys belonging to travelers, maybe even a few camels, perhaps a cow or two used locally to supply milk for inns, some chickens, surely a watchdog, and probably a cat or two. This was hardly the place Mary had pictured as the birthplace for the Son of God. In this setting, who would possibly note the monumental events that were soon to come? Yet a group of men, camping many miles from Bethlehem, had to be completely unprepared for what was about to happen. As they went about their routine, they expected nothing more unusual than maybe a visit from a neighboring shepherd. So being visited by angels must have not only shocked them but scared them to death. We take that facet of the Christmas story for granted now; It seems quaint and appropriate. But considering what the heavenly hosts told these humble men, imagine what must have been going on in these men's minds. They were told that the Son of God had been born, but he was not in a palace surrounded by legions of armies. He was in a barn being watched over by lowly beasts of the field. When put into perspective, being spoken to by an angel on a dark night was surely more believable than being told God's Son was taking his first breaths in a stable. On top of all that, the angels told them to drop what they were doing and go witness this inconceivable event.

A shepherd did not just walk away from his flock. The sheep were the most important things in a shepherd's life. Sheep depended on the men for everything from protection to food. Yet these men did not hesitate. Taking a huge step of faith, they turned their backs on their earthly responsibilities to serve a higher calling, even if that calling, for reasons they could not comprehend, led them to a barn.

The Bible tells us the shepherds were not disappointed that they made the journey. We can sense from what little is written that these men were awed by what they found in that stable. Yet until Bill Gaither walked into a Nashville office and met with songwriters Woody Wright and Michael Sykes, the story of their excitement was a part of that magnificent night in the stable that had been pretty much ignored.

"The Homecoming Friends were scheduled to shoot the videos *Christmas in the Country* and *A Time for Joy* in Birmingham, Alabama," Woody recalled. "I was working for Gaither Music at the time, plugging their catalog to the Nashville music community. That day Bill brought his 'hook book' to my office there on 19th Avenue South, just off music row, and he had Michael bring his keyboard over. We took several of his ideas and gave them musical direction."

Bill wanted the new Christmas songs to have a country feel to them. He also wanted them to be up-tempo and exciting. He wanted the song's themes to be true to biblical history, but also modern and optimistic. Even though Wright and Sykes had not been given insight into the whys of what he wanted to do, the duo knew Gaither had his reasons for creating something that had a very different feel than the normal Christmas anthem or slow-moving carol. As he explained what he wanted from the musical score, Woody and Michael realized they would be creating a sound unlike anything ever performed on the famed Gaither Homecoming videos.

"Christmas can be an extremely sad time," Bill began as he explained his reasoning in wrapping the musical score with a very uplifting tune. "There have been many studies done that point to the fact the suicide rate is the highest during the

Christmas holidays. For that reason, I wanted the two videos we were going to do to have some songs of joy, optimism, and fun. I thought an up-tempo country kind of fun sound would be perfect. After all, the first Christmas was certainly in a rural setting. So we wrote music with that idea in mind. Then Gloria came up with, 'You got to see what's happening in the barn.' I think Gloria's lyrics are fantastic. 'Come and see what's happening in the barn, I've seen nothing like this since I've been on the farm, those strangers camping out there have a baby in their arms, come and see what's happening in the barn.' "

As he spoke, Bill's pride in his wife's catchy lyrics was obvious. But what is most amazing about Gloria's work was how she captured the story of the birth of Christ in a bright new lyrical light. She brought to life the man who owned that stable, showed him meeting the couple, and then had this almost forgotten participant in the first Christmas being awakened by the brightness of the Christmas star. His curiosity piqued, he had to know what was going on. So this man rushed outside into that light and was greeted by music more beautiful than he could imagine. As he drew near his barn, he noted unknown shepherds. They approached him trying to find words to explain their visit from angels. Then they told him that in his very barn the Son of God had just been born.

When it all was said and done, the quartet of writers accomplished Bill's goal of creating a song that embraced the feel of American country music coupled with the very rural story of the birth of God's Son. The final product of this labor of love was as elementary as a folk song and as deeply moving as carols dating back hundreds of years. Besides the biblical story, "Come See What's Happening" also brought out the fact that the holidays were filled with happiness; even today they are a time to reach out and share that joy of the first Christmas with others. Perhaps this message was so strong because Bill knew from firsthand experience that when shared, Christmas could heal even the most deeply injured heart.

The real inspiration for this happy carol had come to Gaither a few years before. A close friend had lost everything he had in just a matter of months. As Christmas approached, the man suddenly found himself with no family, few friends, and a faith unsure that the next day, much less the next year, would offer anything worth the price of trying to fight through this dark period. Sensing the person might not be able to survive the sadness of a lonely holiday, Bill and Gloria asked him to spend Christmas with their family.

At first the man seemed lost and held back from joining the festivities. It was evident the dark clouds of grief were still consuming him. But as carols were sung and stories of Christmases past were shared, a bit of light came back into his eyes. By Christmas dinner the man even found himself smiling. That night he looked over at Bill and said, "I think I'm okay." Time would prove that he had rediscovered his will to live through the process of having a family take him in during the holiday season.

"Christ came to bring people together," Bill explained, "but at the time when we celebrate his birth, many feel the most separated."

With his uplifting and spirited Christmas music, the Grammy-winning writer hopes to change that. By reaching out to those who have no one during the holidays, he feels he is living the first Christmas message in the way Christ directed all Christians to do. As Bill has discovered, when the full ramifications of what happened in the rural setting more than two thousand years ago are realized, it is impossible not to get excited. Two millennia ago, shepherds dropped their most important task to witness the first Christmas. Today it falls to us to share those men's excitement with others by shouting out, "Come and see what's happening in the barn!"

CAROL OF THE BELLS

*I*t is impossible to imagine a Christmas without bells. Church bells, jingle bells, sleigh bells, street-corner Santas ringing bells, and the Salvation Army's bells seem to surround us from Thanksgiving to Christmas day. They ring everywhere, never letting us forget that the holiday season is upon us.

Yet Christmas bells do not end on street corners, in steeples, or jingling on sleighs — that is just where they start. Some of the most treasured Christmas songs, such as "I Heard the Bells on Christmas Day" and "Silver Bells," trumpet the coupling of the holiday season with the pealing of bells. These beloved carols embrace the bell as a musical expression of God's wonder, hope, and love, as well as the triumphant signal for the coming of his Son.

Hollywood has never been shy about employing the symbolism of Christmas bells either. *The Bells of St. Mary*, *The Lemon Drop Kid*, and even *Holiday Inn* focus on bells as a central expression of the spirit of the season. In perhaps the most adored holiday motion picture ever produced, *It's a Wonderful Life*, a ringing bell signals the Lord's mission has been fully accomplished and all is again right in George's world.

As bells are the symbols of joyful chimes announcing important news, such as weddings, the end of wars, and the beginning of new lives, it seems only natural that Christmas is the season when bells are most evident. Could there be a better reason for their chiming than in ringing out the good news of Christ's birth?

While most think of bells in fairly modern terms, history tells us that for hundreds of years bells have been an important and even an essential part of holidays. Even back in the Dark Ages, pealing church bells announced the arrival of each new Christmas day. For generations children have rung handbells as they caroled. In fact there is even a legend that states the bell-ringing tradition actually started on the very first Christmas night.

There are no biblical records of bells ringing when Christ was born. The Gospels of Matthew, Mark, Luke, and John do not mention the use of bells in the manger. Paul never shared the news of ringing bells in any of his letters either. There is actually only one reference to a bell in the entire Bible, and that is found near the end of the book of Zechariah. Yet in spite of the fact it was not chronicled by Gospel writers, there is a story handed down by the early Christians that some accept as true. The tale goes that on that first Christmas, every bell on the face of the earth magically chimed at the same time to welcome God's Son. The narrative further states that never had the earth heard such a majestic and melodious refrain. It seemed the bells rang in perfect harmony, their tones joining in a joyous song of hope and wonder. And supposedly, as the whole world heard those harmonic strains, millions paused to consider the power behind them, while acknowledging the birth of the new king.

As there were few bells and no church towers during the days of Christ, this legend was probably invented hundreds of years after the Savior's birth. Some historians believe it was initially used during holiday church celebrations as a way to get

Hark! how the bells
Sweet silver bells
All seem to say,
"Throw cares away."
Christmas is here
Bringing good cheer
To young and old
Meek and the bold
Ding, dong, ding, dong
That is their song
With joyful ring
All caroling
One seems to hear
Words of good cheer
From ev'rywhere
Filling the air

Oh how they pound,
Raising the sound,
O'er hill and dale,
Telling their tale,
Gaily they ring
While people sing
Songs of good cheer
Christmas is here
Merry, merry, merry, merry
    Christmas
Merry, merry, merry, merry
    Christmas
On, on they send
On without end
Their joyful tone
To ev'ry home

children involved in the pageants. These Christian plays were an important part of worship in the Dark Ages. This legend of the Christmas bells seems to be most deeply rooted in Eastern Europe, where even in the early part of the 1900s the tale was told time and time again. Yet for all the centuries the legend flourished, the story was just that — a story. Though many probably had tried, no one ever managed to compose a melody that captured the harmonic spirit of the old tale. Finally, in 1916, the most popular composer in the Ukraine penned what would become the basis for a song celebrating the sounds made by the tolling of the first Christmas bells.

Mykola Dmytrovich Leontovych was thirty-nine years old and a national celebrity in the Ukraine and Russia when he sat down to compose the music for what has become one of the world's most popular Christmas carols. Yet when he finished his "Shchedryk," it was not yet the holiday song we now know as "Carol of the Bells." While surely based on the legend of the Christmas bells, the writer's new choral piece celebrated the awakening of God's people to the beauty that could be found each day in his creation. So "Shchedryk" was not just a holiday song; it was a piece that could be sung at any time of the year. The fact that Leontovych's masterpiece was first performed by students at Kiev University in December 1916 helped identify it with the Christmas season.

From its debut, "Shchedryk" with its light, airy melody and beautiful harmonies, was embraced and loved by the Ukrainian people. It was performed much like a folk round with three- or four-part harmonies. Though it seemed complicated to those hearing it for the first time, it was surprisingly easy to learn and sing. "Shchedryk" was also a piece that always brought a worshipful response to all who heard it, so it was as well suited for a cathedral as it was a stage or theater. Yet even while choirs around the Ukraine sang it, its peaceful message seemed to be constantly drowned out by events that would change the course of history and severely alter the Ukraine and its people for decades.

When "Shchedryk" was written, the world was experiencing chaotic change. The royal family of Russia was overthrown, Lenin rose to power, the war to end all wars brought the globe to the brink of destruction, and, as a part of the new Soviet empire, Leontovych's beloved Ukraine would all but lose its identity for more than seventy-five years. Perhaps disheartened by these traumatic events, just four years after his masterpiece had been initially performed, the middle-aged writer died in a world he hardly recognized.

Twenty years later, another musical visionary resurrected Leontovych's magical composition. Peter Wilhousky had never been to Eastern Europe, but he understood the region very well. Wilhousky was born in Passaic, New Jersey, but his parents came from what is now known as the Czech Republic. Even though they left Europe to seek out opportunity in the United States, the couple never forgot their Slavic roots. They taught their children the native songs and dances and also shared with them the ancient legends. Therefore the old world music and the folk stories became a part of the boy's essence. It would be those elements of his youth, combined with his talent and experience, that gave birth to the "Carol of the Bells."

Gifted with a beautiful singing voice, at about the same time Leontovych was composing "Shchedryk," Peter was a part of the renowned Russian Cathedral Boys Choir in New York City. The lad was there when the group gave a command performance before President Woodrow Wilson at the White House and sang before crowds numbering in the tens of thousands in New York. Yet these events were just the beginning of an education that led to Wilhousky's receiving a B.A. from what is now known as the Juilliard School of Music.

During his first fifteen years after graduation, Wilhousky created the Mormon Tabernacle Choir's stirring concert arrangement of "The Battle Hymn of the Republic," started and directed the 1,500 voice All City High School Chorus of New York, and produced several major concerts at Carnegie Hall. By 1936, Wilhousky was also the arranger for the famed NBC radio network's symphony orchestra. Yet even with the heavy demands of his schedule and the long list of honors tossed his way, the young composer never quit studying the music of Eastern Europe. This research led to his discovering the beauty of Leontovych's "Shchedryk."

Fascinated by the song's simple tune and elegant harmonies, Wilhousky began to play with the twenty-year-old composition. Soon the composer became convinced that Lenotovych's "Shchedryk" clearly captured the spirit of every bell in the world ringing out in perfect harmony. While keeping the essence and feel of the original work, the American combined the joy found in Leontovych's ringing bells with an old Slavic legend his parents had told many years before. In 1936, with Wilhousky's new lyrics and arrangement, the "Carol of the Bells" was born.

Sparked by a performance on NBC radio, the "Carol of the Bells" rapidly became one of the country's most popular choral pieces. Wilhousky's All City High School Chorus quickly made the carol an essential part of a holiday experience, as did various choirs all over the United States. Remarkably, within two decades the "Carol of the Bells" had been performed millions of times, recorded thousands of times, and translated into scores of different languages. Only a handful of other holiday songs had ever found universal acceptance as swiftly as the "Carol of the Bells."

A thousand years ago almost every child in Central and Eastern Europe knew the story of the legend of the bells. That tale has all but been forgotten now, but the song it inspired has become one of the most beautiful tributes to the true spiritual joy of the holiday season. In an era when holiday bells often are not harmonious and ring for reasons that have little to do with the events of the first Christmas, the "Carol of the Bells" reminds all of us of the harmony that comes when the Lord enters not only the world but also our hearts.

LITTLE DRUMMER BOY

atherine Davis lived eighty-eight years and during that
time wrote more than one thousand pieces of music.
A piano teacher at Wellesley College, her work as a
composer would earn her an honorary doctorate from Stetson
University and a writing award from the American Society of
Composers, Artists, and Publishers. Yet while thousands of
choirs performed Davis's cantatas, while millions have heard
her choral anthems, she is best remembered today for a single
song — a very simple carol penned in the months preceding
World War II.

Katherine Davis was born in 1892 in St. Joseph, Missouri.
Katherine so loved music that from childhood she saw the
world in melody and verse. A student of history, Davis spent
time learning both American and European folk music. Combined with the choral anthems she sang in church and school,
these influences led to Katherine's developing a musical style
that was rich in content and harmonization. So unique and
accomplished were her original pieces that, while she was still
a young woman, Davis earned the praise of a host of music
publishers and critics. She also grew used to hearing choirs
sing her best work.

Driven to penning as many as two or three songs a week,
Davis was constantly searching for new inspiration. She read
the Bible, history books, and even children's fairy tales. She

especially was drawn to folk legends. She even adapted several of these into songs and musical plays. It was probably in an ancient European story that she uncovered the inspiration for what would become her most beloved work.

There are many French and English folktales concerning gifts given to the baby Jesus. These touching stories of poor people sharing what little they had to celebrate and honor the Lord's birth have been passed down for hundreds of years. Yet in the Great Depression, these tales of seemingly unworthy gifts given from the heart being magnified into something wondrous meant more than they ever before had. In a world where tens of millions couldn't even afford to buy a Christmas card, a gift from the heart was now all they had to offer their friends and families.

There can be little doubt that Katherine understood the suffering that was all around her. She no doubt witnessed poor children peering through toy-shop windows at the same time fathers and mothers were being forced to make presents out of leftover pieces of twine, wood, and ribbon. She had to wonder if these handmade gifts would bring joy or disappointment on Christmas morning.

The third variable that probably moved Davis to pen her most famous Christmas ode was the looming threat of another World War. Even before the attack on Pearl Harbor, there was a somber mood in almost every church service, radio news report, and newspaper story. The world was on the brink of self-destruction, everyone knew about it, and there appeared to be no way to avoid the conflict.

With these thoughts in mind, Davis, who most often penned complex and intricate musical pieces, sat down at the piano in 1941 and wrote a very simple song about a very unpretentious Christmas gift. Imagining a poor child coming to witness the birth of the Savior, Katherine composed "The Carol of the Drum."

The child who was the focal point of Davis's song might have been from ancient Israel, but in 1941 he could have come off the streets of any American town. He was a victim of poverty, a polite child whose only possession was a small drum. All he could offer was to "play his best." But before he began, still very unsure that what he was offering was good enough for a king, the small boy asked Mary if his gift would be appropriate. It was the story that millions knew well in the days of economic chaos and impending war. After all, it was a time when peace on earth seemed like a fairy tale.

Even though its message seemed so much a part of the times, "The Carol of the Drum," spurred on by its elementary percussion beat, did not become one of the songs that inspired a world at war. Like thousands of other Christmas carols, it was pushed aside. During these years Americans instead clung to sentimental numbers such as "I'll Be Home for Christmas" and "White Christmas." In fact it seemed the holidays of World War II had less to do with the gospel found in Luke and much more to do with families praying to be safely reunited for a future Christmas Day. So for almost two decades, "The Carol of the Drum" remained an unknown melody with a forgotten message. During this time, Katherine moved on to other types of music and messages.

In 1958, Harry Simeone, while searching for ideas for a Christmas album, happened upon Davis's carol. Simeone had once directed the famed Fred Waring Orchestra. He now had his own choir. Sensing that voices could blend to produce a drum beat, the choir leader dusted off the World War II reject. He then rearranged Davis's "Carol of the Drum," renamed it, and took it to the recording studio. Convinced this song was a hit, in November the Harry Simeone Chorale's "Little Drummer Boy" was released. In the era of rock and roll, doo-wop, and teen idols, the Christmas story of a poor child and his drum took the nation by storm.

By 1962, "Little Drummer Boy" had been recorded more than a hundred times and had appeared on the pop charts on five occasions. The song had also been featured on countless television shows and was being adapted into an animated movie starring Greer Garson. By the end of the decade, only two other Christmas songs, "White Christmas" and "Rudolf the Red-Nosed Reindeer," had generated more success.

No one was more shocked by the public's response to her "Carol of the Drum" than was Katherine Davis. At the age of seventy, after working for more than five decades in relative obscurity, she was suddenly in the nation's spotlight. Her story of a child who played drums for the baby Jesus would keep Davis in the nation's heart until her death in 1980.

Katherine Davis could not explain why "Little Drummer Boy" came to mean so much to America. Perhaps a part of it was due to the climate that had enveloped the nation the year Harry Simeone recorded the song. For the first time people were faced with the prospect that man had the power to blow the earth apart with the push of a button. The fear of nuclear bombs ending time itself caused many to yearn for an era when peace on earth came down to something far less complex than a United Nations debate or an Iron Curtain separating good from bad and right from wrong. So the carol that had been written on the eve of the Second World War became a prayer for peace during the height of the Cold War. Maybe, some thought, if the leaders of the world would simply listen to the hearts and minds of the children, then peace would be deemed more important than territorial or political disputes. Perhaps a single drum played with sincerity could silence the angry voices long enough to focus on the real reason for celebrating Christmas.

Simple, direct, and honest, "Little Drummer Boy" might have been based on a legend, but in its verses are beautiful examples of the best Christmas gift of all — a rich present wrapped in love and delivered by a child.

I SAW THREE SHIPS

I Saw Three Ships" proves that even a carol based on faith doesn't necessarily have to make a great deal of sense to be popular. Once known as "Christmas Day in the Morning," this old song jumbles truth in such a confusing manner that today most sing it with no clue of its real meaning. Yet in spite of the fact that sailing to Bethlehem makes absolutely no sense, with its upbeat, bouncing melody, "I Saw Three Ships" has somehow retained its popularity as a Christmas classic. So even though no one really understands why, the carol still rings true with those who celebrate the true meaning of Christmas.

A popular Scottish song from the sixteenth century was probably at least a part of the inspiration for "I Saw Three Ships." A stanza in the old folk number echoed a bit of the carol's biblical theme.

> *There comes a ship far sailing then,*
> *Saint Michael was the stieres-man;*
> *Saint John sate in the horn:*
> *Our Lord harped, and Lady sang.*
> *And all the bells of heaven they rang,*
> *On Christ's Sonday at morn.*

While it is fairly easy to see the similarity between the Scottish religious number and the carol, in a modern world it still seems strange to connect the birth of Christ to an ocean voyage. To understand why Mary sailed to Bethlehem, one must look at a mix of British history, European legend, and sixteenth-century pop culture.

During the 1600s, the English were completely caught up in the lore of the sea. This was the dawning of a new age. Columbus had discovered America only two hundred years before, thereby opening up the oceans for exploration. By this time many British sailors had actually journeyed all over the globe, bringing back tales of their adventures. A few courageous men and women had even attempted to colonize the New World. So tales of the sea were the main topics of conversation in pubs and in parlors, as well as on farms and in castles. Ocean adventures were written into bestselling books, stage plays, and children's stories. There were tales of ships that left port but never came home. Some, like the *Flying Dutchman*, seemed destined to sail the seas until judgment day. Little boys went to sleep at night dreaming of sailing the open seas, fighting unknown monsters, discovering new lands, and finding riches beyond compare. Yet even to a nation that could boast the greatest fleet in the world and whose people took great pride in ruling the world's waves, creating a song about sailing to Jesus' birth still seems a stretch.

"I Saw Three Ships" was obviously composed by a person who lacked formal education. Master hymn writer and theologian Charles Wesley would never have conceived an image of three ships sailing into landlocked Bethlehem. Wesley based his works on a strict interpretation of Scripture. Yet in the fifteenth century only a few English men and women could read, and almost no one had access to a Bible. As most church services were conducted in Latin, a language the common man did not speak, God's Word was a mystery. With this in mind, if the writer lived in a sea port and was immersed in the lore of the ocean and exploration, as most were during this period, then naturally he or she probably pictured most biblical cities located on bodies of water.

During this same period there were many stories circulated about how the remains of the wise men had been taken from the Holy Land to Constantinople, then to Milan, and finally Cologne. These bodies, along with a number of relics from Christ's birth, supposedly arrived in Germany by ship in 1162. By the 1600s this legend was very well known in England and thus offered another tie to the sea and figures who were an important facet of the story of Christ's birth. Even though the Bible makes no reference to the number of wise men who came to honor the baby Jesus, by this time most had come to believe the number was three because of the number of gifts that were brought. Yet in England the three wise men might also have been tied to the fact that this was the number of ships that, legend had it, arrived in Cologne with their remains.

Though no published manuscripts survive, it is believed the initial version of "I Saw Three Ships" was composed about the journey of the wise men's bodies from the Holy Land to Cologne. This first song might even have been written in Eastern Europe, but at some point an English man or woman decided to use the framework of this legend to tell the story of the birth of Christ in the "port of Bethlehem." During a period when carols were not sung in the Church of England, the song became very popular with the nation's rural poor.

As time passed, children began to ask questions about why there was a trio of ships but only two people, Jesus and Mary, sailing on them. This is when the ships began to take on meanings of their own. In some towns the trio represented faith, hope, and charity. In other communities it was explained that Joseph was on the third ship, but he was not mentioned in the song. A final explanation that pointed toward the purpose of Christ's life and his resurrection was that the three vessels represented God the Father, Son, and Holy Spirit.

I saw three ships come sailing in
On Christmas Day, on Christmas Day;
I saw three ships come sailing in
On Christmas Day in the morning.
And what was in those ships all three,
On Christmas Day, on Christmas Day?
And what was in those ships all three,
On Christmas Day in the morning?
The Virgin Mary and Christ were there,
On Christmas Day, on Christmas Day;
The Virgin Mary and Christ were there,
On Christmas Day in the morning.
Pray, whither sailed those ships all three,
On Christmas Day, on Christmas Day?
Pray, whither sailed those ships all three,
On Christmas Day in the morning?
O they sailed into Bethlehem,
On Christmas Day, on Christmas Day;

O they sailed into Bethlehem,
On Christmas Day in the morning.
And all the bells on earth shall ring,
On Christmas Day, on Christmas Day;
And all the bells on earth shall ring,
On Christmas Day in the morning.
And all the angels in heaven shall sing,
On Christmas Day, on Christmas Day;
And all the angels in heaven shall sing,
On Christmas Day in the morning.
And all the souls on earth shall sing,
On Christmas Day, on Christmas Day;
And all the souls on earth shall sing,
On Christmas Day in the morning.
Then let us all rejoice again,
On Christmas Day, on Christmas Day;
Then let us all rejoice again,
On Christmas Day in the morning.

With the creation of the King James Bible, most Christians began to develop a much clearer image of the geography of the Holy Land. As they did, believers began to understand that normal ships could not sail across Middle Eastern sands and grass lands to Bethlehem. Yet rather than give up their favorite Christmas carol, the people of England ascribed magical powers to the vessels. In the minds of those who sang "I Saw Three Ships," God could easily make a vessel travel over dry ground. And so the carol survived.

While few today can truly relate to this old carol's imagery and while much of "I Saw Three Ships" has little connection with the actual biblical story of Christ's birth, the song nevertheless hits some chords that do reflect much of the genuine meaning of Christmas. A great part of that can be found in the carol's spirit.

It is a happy song, one that immediately catches singers up in the joy of the moment. Its message might not be accurate in many ways, but the writer did understand that God's Son was miraculously born to a virgin. And even though that happened long ago in a faraway place called Bethlehem, the songwriter also realized this birth was still very important to those who lived in England. As bells in the 1600s always rang to signal important news in a community, the writer sensed that all the bells on earth must have rung out proclaiming the Savior's birth. And then, even though the person who created the lyrics had probably never read from the Bible, they understood that angels would lend their voices to announce the world's greatest event. Naturally, all of the earth's people would join with the heavenly hosts in song as well.

"I Saw Three Ships" was married to a wonderfully bouncy tune that is thought to be a traditional English melody. Some historians trace its origin to the town of Derbyshire. The tune and words were first published together in 1833 in William Sandy's *Christmas Carols, Ancient and Modern*.

"I Saw Three Ships" is simple, direct, and only remotely tied to reality. Yet when viewed through the writer's eyes, the old carol takes on a special imagery and meaning. As surely as England's ships could be seen sailing back home after a long journey, the participants in the first Christmas could be seen in the eyes of one who had the faith to look for them. Even today, with enough faith, carolers can still see that vision and understand its power.

WE NEED A LITTLE CHRISTMAS

ew York City at Christmas is hardly the image projected by a Currier and Ives holiday illustration, Charles Dickens' *A Christmas Carol*, or the Hollywood seasonal classic *It's a Wonderful Life*. Yet for many Americans it is in the Big Apple where the holidays seem to be most alive.

No one can argue that December in New York is a very special time. The city lays claim to the huge tree in Rockefeller Center, Radio City Music Hall's famed Rockettes, thousands of stores and shops incredibly decorated for the Christmas season, graceful skaters in Central Park, seemingly limitless shoppers strolling on Park Avenue, and the hundreds of picturesque horse-drawn carriages giving rides to those fully infected with Christmas spirit along the busy streets. Yet in spite of these poetic images, few Christmas songs have their roots in America's biggest city. Yes, "Silver Bells" owes its life to New York's red and green traffic lights, and "It's Beginning to Look a Lot Like Christmas" made its debut here as well, but most other holiday carols embrace more rural settings or the images of Christ in the manger.

Though most Americans don't realize it, there is a modern Christmas favorite that was sung every day for more than four years in New York City. Remarkably that song's spirited message is more alive now than it was when Angela Lansbury first performed it on a Broadway stage on May 24, 1966. And while that date is the beginning of this famous song's immense popularity, the beginning of the story behind the song got its start more than three decades earlier.

In 1933, in the midst of the Great Depression, Jerry Herman was born in New York City. Even during this nation's darkest days, Herman was fortunate to be raised by musically inclined teachers who had the money to give their son piano lessons and take him to see Broadway musicals. In the midst of the worst economic period in America's history, Jerry's folks brought to his life a sense of optimistic promise. Yet even though his home was filled with laughter and hope, he could not fully escape the pain that was all around him. Beginning four years before his birth, with the stock market's crash and going on through World War II, these were tough times for most families, and Herman knew it. The older he grew, the more he realized that this was an era when nightmares and dreams often collided. For most it was a time when Christmas was a holiday filled with great wishes but few presents.

The United States was saving the world from Hitler when as a teen at the Stissing Lake Camp in the Berkshire Mountains Jerry directed both *Finian's Rainbow* and *A Tree Grows in Brooklyn*. For young Herman the Broadway bug that bit him at that camp would forever change his life. The magical music, the merging of talents, the creative mix of acting and singing, and the sound of applause provided the youth with a vehicle with which he could bring joy to others. Hearing a call, Jerry gave his life to the theater.

Not satisfied to work with existing productions, even before he finished high school Herman began to write songs and draft plays. He continued to compose and create throughout his days as a student at the University of Miami. Graduating from college at twenty-one with his eyes set on a goal, Jerry returned to New York. Within months Herman's *I Feel Wonderful* opened in Greenwich Village. Beginning on October

18, 1954, the musical ran for forty-eight performances. While *Wonderful* might not have been a great success, it did open the door for the "Boy Wonder." Theaters and backers were ready to give the "kid" a chance.

Within seven years Herman had a legitimate Broadway hit with *Milk and Honey*. Yet it would be his third show, *Hello Dolly!*, that would make him the toast of the Great White Way. The original production, starring Carol Channing, ran for 2,844 performances from January 16, 1964 to December 27, 1970. *Hello Dolly!* remains one of the most beloved stage musicals of all time. A string of other hits would follow *Dolly*, and soon the writer would even find his work produced for the Hollywood screen. Yet for more than just his musicals, Jerry was known for the power of the songs inside those plays.

Herman's individual numbers had a rich life well beyond the New York stage, more so than those of any Broadway composer. While few outside of the Big Apple ever heard most Broadway show tunes, Jerry's became pop standards. The title cut from *Hello Dolly!* was a monster hit for Louis Armstrong. Eydie Gorme won a Grammy with "If He Walked into My Life." More than a dozen other Herman-penned Broadway standards found their way out of his shows and onto the pop charts. The much-honored member of the Songwriters Hall of Fame and the Theatre Hall of Fame once said he was most proud of having written songs that could have lives of their own outside of his stage productions. Yet even with this unique success, little did the song scribe realize when creating the Broadway smash *Mame* that one of his numbers would become a universally acclaimed holiday standard.

Jerry Herman's *Mame* premiered at the Winter Garden Theatre in New York City on May 24, 1966. The musical was based on a play by Jerome Lawrence and Robert E. Lee. Before that it had been a successful novel by Patrick Dennis. The book, play, and musical all centered on the tale of an eclectic woman who lived in luxury on New York City's Upper East Side. Within the themes running through the book and play, Herman sensed a chance to create a bright comedy filled with unique characters.

Even before *Mame* premiered, everyone from stage critics to Broadway fans expected it to be the season's biggest hit. The main reason cited for this rosy forecast was simply that "if Jerry Herman wrote it, then it has to be great." Yet what no one expected on that late spring night was to leave the theater singing an incredibly optimistic Christmas song. Yet that is exactly what happened.

"We Need a Little Christmas" made its appearance about midway through the play. The scene was framed by the cast of characters coming to grips with the stock market crash of 1929. With doom and gloom all around her, Mame somehow found reason to hope and declared the need for a little Christmas spirit right this very minute. She seemed to believe that the Christmas spirit would help to bring back the happiness dashed by Wall Street's blackest day. So with a smile on her face and a spring in her step, Mame cried out for everyone to "haul out the holly" and "fill up the stocking," and then added a plea for Santa to make his rounds early as "Santa, dear, we're in a hurry."

When writing *Mame*, Herman sensed that the scenes after the fall of the stock market needed to lift people up by turning a tragedy into a triumph. This was not an original idea. As he was growing up in New York City, the writer had noted that Christmas had been able to transform lives and moods even in the midst of the uncertainty of the Depression and World War II. As Herman wrote in his autobiography, "You don't have to wait for a special day to celebrate Christmas. It was more important to celebrate Christmas when you need it." For his lead character, Mame, this was a time that cried out for Christmas.

Jerry, who often spent months perfecting his music, admitted that "We Need A Little Christmas" was easy to write because it "brought out inner strengths in that woman that she didn't even know she had — that I didn't even know she had." What the composer could not have realized at the time was how much the world yearned for Mame's upbeat message of hope.

Just as it had been on Black Tuesday and throughout the Great Depression, 1966 was a part of an era steeped in uncertainty. The Vietnam War, the riots over the struggle for racial equality, the integration of schools, the assassination of prominent politicians and social leaders, the threat of another world war, this time with the Soviet Union, and the message that "God was dead" had everyone on pins and needles. Many honestly felt the best days of the country had passed and the last days of the earth were just ahead. Few were optimistic and hardly anyone was preaching that the world was filled with blessings. Then came Herman's song.

"We Need a Little Christmas" struck a mighty chord that night on Broadway and five months later in America. Recorded by Andy Williams, Julius La Rosa, and the New Christy Minstrels, the song found instant airplay on radio stations in late November of 1966. It was a song with easy-to-remember lyrics, an unforgettable tune, and a message that erased doubts and created smiles. Because of the perfect marriage of music and message, just as had happened with "White Christmas" in 1944, "We Need a Little Christmas" became an immediate classic.

In the middle of the uncertain 1960s, Mame's message of needing "a little angel" was one almost everyone could embrace. Therefore, for at least a few minutes, the cheery "We Need A Little Christmas" brought hope to a world filled with darkness and quieted the loud voices of doom. Though it's not a song that touches on the gospel of Christ in the manger, "We Need a

Little Christmas" nevertheless echoes the faith needed to make it through uncertain times. So in a very real sense, this Broadway show tune captured the spirit of Christmas like few secular songs ever have. Part prayer, mixed with a portion of cheerleading and a cry for faith, "We Need a Little Christmas" is a timeless reminder of why the holidays are so important to so many.

Blue Christmas

s usual, Jay Johnson was running late. He had been slow getting started that morning, and the cold rainy weather wasn't helping at all. On top of that, his green 1939 Mercury convertible had developed a huge rip just above the driver's seat, and water was pouring through the growing hole onto his head. Pulling the car off to the side of the road, the forty-five-year-old Johnson rummaged among the papers he kept in his backseat until he found an umbrella. He pushed it through the hole in the canvas top, then hit the button to open the umbrella. Shifting into first gear, he eased the car back onto the road, with the umbrella keeping most of the water out of the car. Jay continued on to the Stamford, Connecticut, train station.

A script and commercial-jingle writer for radio, Johnson was on his way to New York, a daily commute that included a one-hour train junket. It was during these trips that Jay would catch up on the postwar news in the paper, work word puzzles, and scribble down inspiration for storylines and songs. His daughter remembers her father as a man driven by creative challenges.

"He often wrote or worked as he rode on the trains," recalled Judy Olmsted. "I am sure that if he were alive today he would have had a laptop computer. He loved to play with words. He made up all kinds of limericks and poems. He wrote for some of the top shows on radio and later on television too. He was a vaudeville veteran, played around with Broadway shows, and even published dozens of songs. Some of their titles were almost as funny as the lyrics. They included 'Peaceful,' 'Little Wedding Bells,' 'Telephone Fever,' 'Sunday Afternoon,' and one of my favorites, 'Peter Pan the Meter Man.' That title alone tells you how his mind worked."

On this particular rainy day, as the train chugged toward the Big Apple, Johnson pulled out an old piece of hotel stationery. The holiday season was just around the corner, and tunes like Irving Berlin's "White Christmas" were being written into many of the radio shows for which he worked. As Jay considered the long list of Christmas classics he could draw from for his scripts, an original idea began to take shape. At first glance it seemed almost too obvious. With the success of "White Christmas" and the tremendous impact of blues music during the forties, surely, Johnson thought, someone had combined the two concepts into a song. A number about a blue Christmas seemed so natural. Yet as he considered the idea, he suddenly and happily realized that no one had yet tackled this play on words. Picking up a pen, he scribbled down his first thoughts.

> I expect to have a colorful Christmas
> tinged with every kind of holiday hue,
> and though I know I'll find every shade
> in the rainbow,
> this design of mine will be mostly blue.

These lines were destined to become the rough first verse of a lyric sheet which Johnson would call "Blue Christmas." Over the course of the next few days, several more verses followed.

Though Christmas is considered a wonderful time by most, it is also a very difficult time for many. Being alone during a holiday period when family and giving are so important would be tough enough without being bombarded at every turn by the very happy and joyful nature of Christmas. So while Christmas brings real happiness and anticipation to millions, Jay Johnson's verses spoke to those forgotten souls who would face the holiday season alone.

Once Jay was satisfied with all his words and seemed assured that he had written something special, he met with friend and composer Billy Hayes. Though no one recalls, Hayes probably offered a few suggestions about the lyrics. Before the two men finished the song, Johnson's first two verses were dropped. Using the writer's later lines, Billy neatly wrapped the package with an appropriate musical score. The finished product was then sold to Choice Music.

"Blue Christmas" was copyrighted in 1948, and Choice Music immediately began to shop their new holiday number. As a novelty and hillbilly specialty company, Choice most likely attempted to interest a number of Nashville artists in "Blue Christmas." Yet no one in Music City noted the song's potential and jumped on board. The first act to record the tune was a pop band, Hugo Winterhalter and His Orchestra.

Winterhalter had worked as an arranger for the likes of Count Basie, Tommy and Jimmy Dorsey, and Claude Thornhill before putting together his own group. In late 1949 he hit the charts for the first time with "Jealous Heart." When he recorded the Johnson-Hayes holiday offering in the early winter, Columbia hoped that it would land their new star in the top ten. Hugo's "Blue Christmas" did just that, topping out at number nine. A year later the song would undertake another successful run up the pop charts for the band leader. Still, these modest numbers didn't forecast a long run on the hit parade. At that time, in terms of recognition and popularity, "Blue Christmas" was far behind holiday standards such as "Silver Bells," "White Christmas," "Rudolph the Red-Nosed Reindeer," and "I'll Be Home for Christmas." Most felt it would soon be forgotten.

Ernest Tubb must have heard the song during its initial Winterhalter release, because the Texas Troubadour worked it into his act at about that time. A year later, in 1950, he cut the number for Decca and took it to the top of the country charts. For the next five years, "Blue Christmas" would become Tubb's holiday theme song and standard hit fodder for country radio playlists.

With its lonesome message and clever lyrics, "Blue Christmas" was truly a hillbilly ode. It may have been written on an East Coast commuter train, but when Tubb vocalized it, it seemed to owe a great deal more to Nashville than New York. So many people identified it with Ernest Tubb that he was often referred to as the "Blue Christmas" writer. While he had contributed nothing to the song's lyrics or score, Tubb had put it on the map and shaped it into a country music standard. Because of the tall Texan, "Blue Christmas" became country music's first true Christmas classic.

By the midfifties almost every country act was using "Blue Christmas" in their November and December shows. While still performed from time to time in pop music, by the late fifties the Johnson-Hayes number had seemingly established itself as a country epic. It was one song that had put some twang in the mistletoe. "Blue Christmas" probably would have remained strictly a part of the Music City genre if not for a young singer who had grown up idolizing Ernest Tubb.

Elvis Presley had listened to a lot of black blues and white Southern gospel during his youth, but he had also spent a great deal of time checking out country acts. The one and only time he worked the *Grand Ole Opry*, he had even met a childhood hero, Ernest Tubb. It was probably Presley's affection for Tubb and his music that led Elvis to record "Blue Christmas" on his initial holiday album. Yet Elvis's cut was far different from Tubb's or anyone else's. The rocker was the first to put real blues in "Blue Christmas." In one brief three-minute recording, Ernest had lost his lock on the song. It was now Elvis's Christmas standard.

Presley's recording of Johnson and Hayes's song would generate more royalties than all of Jay Johnson's other songs combined. It would also assure that this country classic would become one of the best known holiday songs of all time. Since Elvis first cut it, "Blue Christmas" has been recorded by hundreds of artists from every musical genre. Yet in spite of its success in rock, pop, and blues, by and large "Blue Christmas" has remained as country as Ernest Tubb. It would be hard to imagine a country Christmas album or show without it. And for that reason, the Jay Johnson and Billy Hayes song has become the gift that keeps on giving.

"I will tell you this," Judy Olmsted said with a laugh, "it wouldn't be Christmas at our house without 'Blue Christmas.'" And a host of country music fans would probably agree that while there are a lot of great secular holiday songs, a real country Christmas isn't complete until it's sung blue.

C–H–R–I–S–T–M–A–S

oday the only live national radio show featuring regular musical performances is the *Grand Ole Opry*. Yet in the first generation of radio, a host of clear-channel stations presented country music variety shows that beamed the music weekly across the entire nation. One of the best came not from the South but the Midwest. If Chicago's *National Barn Dance* had not spotlighted hillbilly or western music each weekend, then the world would have probably never known the likes of Rex Allen, Pat Buttram, Red Foley, Patsy Montana, Gene Autry, Eddie Arnold, and a host of other hall of fame acts. And without the *Barn Dance*, America would not have been given a wonderful carol known by many as the "Christmas alphabet song."

During its initial week, WLS had devoted much of its schedule to classical music. For a joke, the manager decided to air an hour of old-time folk performances on the station's first Saturday night. On April 19, 1924, WLS Radio's *National Barn Dance* debuted. Though the Sears-Roebuck management was aghast by this "disgraceful lowbrow music," the public was entranced. Scores of telegrams poured in demanding more of these hillbilly strains. So the program did not just continue, it thrived. By 1931 the *National Barn Dance* was drawing sold-out crowds to the Eighth Street Theatre every Saturday night for the program's live 7:30 and 10:00 shows. The broadcast became so popular that the NBC radio network picked it up the next year. A national sponsor, Miles Laboratories, soon assured the performers solid ratings and bigger paychecks.

That same year the *Barn Dance* went coast to coast, Evelyn, Eva, and Lucille Overstake made the trip from Decatur to Chicago to audition for a spot on the program. Their rural harmonies made a big impression on the producers, and the "Three Little Maids" earned a place on the musical extravaganza. Eventually the guitar-playing Maid, Lucille, spun off on her own, changed her name to Jenny Lou Carson, and by World War II emerged as one of WLS's biggest stars.

Though Carson would garner some recording with Decca and RCA Victor, it would be her songwriting where she made her biggest mark on both country and popular music. The pretty brunette penned such classics as "Jealous Heart," "Chained to a Memory," "I'll Trade All My Tomorrows," and "Don't Rob Another Man's Castle." A host of stars including Tex Ritter, Gene Autry, Hank Thompson, Jim Reeves, Kay Starr, Patti Page, and Bing Crosby put their spin on Carson tunes. Yet the man who usually scored the biggest with Jenny Lou's work was another *Barn Dance* regular, Eddy Arnold.

Raised on a Tennessee farm, Arnold landed his first radio gig in Memphis before World War II. His smooth voice and casual stage manner captured the bookers' imaginations. He was soon touring the nation with Pee Wee King's Golden West Cowboys and Minnie Pearle. This troupe performed for U.S. servicemen throughout America during the war. In 1945, Arnold, now a feature act on the *National Barn Dance*, released his first of more than eighty hit singles for RCA. "That's How Much I Love You" began a string of chart toppers that included "It's a Sin," "I'll Hold You in My Heart (Till I Can Hold You in My Arms)," "Anytime," "What a Fool I Was," "Texarkana Baby," "Just a Little Lovin' (Will Go a Long, Long Way)," and "Bouquet of Roses."

As a regular on powerful WLS, Arnold was given huge exposure each Saturday night. With his smooth style, the singer took country to the city and even toured Europe. Thanks to that exposure, a new generation of hits followed, topping the charts in the United States and around the world. Arnold was country music's first international superstar.

While working together on WLS, Eddy and Jenny Lou became good friends. The two visited between shows, and Arnold was often the first to hear Carson's latest compositions. In 1949, during one of their many conversations, Jenny Lou mentioned a phone call she had recently received. A friend had suggested that Carson pen a Christmas song around the theme of the nine letters in the word *Christmas*. It is doubtful that either Jenny Lou or Eddy knew Christmas was derived from Christ Mass, or the worship of Christ. At the time, few Protestant laypeople connected the word *mass*, which they thought of only as a Catholic church service, with the name of the holy day set aside to remember and celebrate Christ's birth. Yet as they talked about putting a new spin on the holidays, both felt a need to keep the song spiritual. Tossing ideas back and forth, the pair began to put together the basis for what many now call the "Christmas Alphabet Carol."

In the late forties the commercial Christmas had really exploded. Montgomery Ward, Sears, J. C. Penney, and others annually printed millions of their Christmas catalogs, and children could hardly wait to get their hands on them. In the days before Wal-Mart and Target, kids would study these wish books for weeks and go to bed each night dreaming of receiving one or more of the toys spotlighted in those catalog's pages. Arnold had observed this many times. It was Eddy who came up with the song's beginning. Therefore he felt that giving the number an introduction centering around a child's view of Christmas was a must. So it was probably Eddy who created the lyrical image of a child whose head was so filled with holiday wishes that he had forgotten about the real reason for the season.

To set up the spelling out of the letters of Christmas, Arnold and Carson then had the child remember what his mother had told him about what the holiday really meant. This memory set up the tagline, "And taught me to spell Christmas this way."

As the two went to work on the alphabet segment of the song, the meaning of "C" was obvious. It stood for Christ and his humble birth. The "H" fell in place as the duo thought of the herald angels who announced the Son of God's coming to the shepherds. "R" was conceived as a bookend to the birth of a Savior, and that would be his crucifixion and resurrection. Eddy and Jenny Lou opted to complete the story of Christ's life by having that letter stand for redeemer. They then decided to use Israel and its place in this biblical story for the "I," and followed with the star that marked where Christ had been born to stand for the fifth letter in Christmas, the "S."

Eddy and Jenny Lou decided the "T" was to stand for the three wise men. This "three" was probably inspired by the song "We Three Kings of Orient Are." In truth, the Bible never actually states how many wise men there were, but most, like Arnold and Carson, rarely realize this, so three is the number locked into most believers' heads.

The "M" of course stood for the manger. The "A" became the inclusive "all" the good things Jesus represented in life and death, and all that he could mean to his followers. The writers closed the letter portion by saluting the humble shepherds. "C-H-R-I-S-T-M-A-S" ultimately concludes with the line, "And that's why there's a Christmas day."

Though it hardly goes into the theological depths that Charles Wesley or Isaac Watts would have explored in creating a hymn, the song really echoed the strong Christian faith of both Carson and Arnold — faith that the duo showed for the remainder of their careers in the gospel songs they sang during their concerts and on their records, as well as in the manner in which they lived their lives. It also reflected what they felt was the most valuable element of the holiday season. So it was a proud moment in April of 1949 when Eddy cut "C-H-R-I-S-T-M-A-S" at the RCA studios in New York.

The Tennessee Plowboy introduced the song to the world that November. In short order the carol would climb into the top ten on *Billboard*'s country charts. Though it would become Eddy's signature holiday song, a host of others quickly jumped on the bandwagon and cut the simple children's carol. Jim Reeves, Rosemary Clooney, Perry Como, Kitty Wells, Andy Williams, Ernest Tubb, Hank Snow, and even the great gospel singer George Beverly Shea all recorded "C-H-R-I-S-T-M-A-S." The song never went out of style either. It remained a popular seasonal commodity as the years rolled by, used in numerous TV specials as well as scores of church musicals. Just when many had forgotten the carol, Bill Gaither revived the Eddy Arnold – Jenny Lou Carson holiday offering. The legendary gospel writer found that modern audiences could still identify with the song that so perfectly reflected a child's view in the years shortly after the end of World War II.

The way people celebrate the holidays has changed a great deal over the centuries. New traditions have been added, the season has become a billion-dollar commercial bonanza for many, Christmas catalogs are largely a thing of the past, and few even remember the *National Barn Dance*. Yet after the gifts have been opened and Christmas wishes have seemingly again been realized, for those who don't know the full meaning of the holiday there is often an emptiness. A simple song, inspired by a phone call, a child's Christmas dreams, and the faith of two entertainers gave birth to a holiday alphabet carol. Even in this modern age, Jenny Lou Carson and Eddy Arnold's simple "C-H-R-I-S-T-M-A-S" really does complete the holiday message by answering why there is a Christmas day.

AULD LANG SYNE/
CHRISTMAS AULD LANG SYNE

uld Lang Syne" is one of the most familiar songs on the planet. It seems that everyone in almost every corner of the world can sing a few of the lines and hum the entire melody. Yet this traditional New Year's anthem was not considered a holiday song until December 31, 1929. On that date Guy Lombardo and His Royal Canadians played the number at a huge New Year's dance. New York's famed Waldorf Astoria Hotel had been booked for the Canadians' big show, a national radio link had been set up to capture the festivities and beam them across the nation, and just before the ringing out of the old year, Lombardo picked up his baton and signaled for his group to launch into "Auld Lang Syne." Thanks to an orchestra leader's choice, suddenly millions of Americans had the mistaken impression that legendary English poet Robert Burns had penned "Auld Lang Syne" just to welcome in the New Year.

Lombardo had first heard the tune in the early twenties while he was on a tour of England. He knew little about the song's history but thought the melody would make a great sentimental number for his orchestra. In his mind it was a great slow-dance song. From at least the midtwenties on, the Royal Canadians had been playing a slow, weepy version of "Auld

Lang Syne" during all of their performances. Though Lombardo's continued use of Burns's song would not change on New Year's Eve 1929, the song's meaning would be forever altered.

"Auld Lang Syne" was probably chosen as the lead-up number to the New Year's countdown because of the nation's bleak mood. In 1929, the stock market had crashed and the economy had fallen into disarray. Fortunes had been lost, people were out of work, and no one seemed to be able to stop the country's descent into a great depression. For Lombardo, a song that embraced the importance and value of friendships over worldly possessions seemed a perfect way to look back and find good things in a very bad year, while looking forward to a new decade that offered more hope. It could be assured that on that night the bandleader had no clue he was creating a holiday tradition that would be going strong in the next century.

Though few who sing it realize it, in Scottish, "Auld Lang Syne" means "old long ago." Elements of the song's origin can be traced back to the 1500s. Sometime in the next century, Sir Robert Ayton wrote a poem that began "Should auld acquaintance be forgot." Though Ayton's composition centered on a love gone bad, much of the poem's mood would later be found in Burns's work, including the final line, "On old-long-syne."

In 1694, in a publication called *Scotch Presbyterian Eloquence Display'd*, a sermon was quoted. In this Sunday morning homily, God said, "Jonah, now billy Jonah, wilt thou go to Ninevah, for Auld lang syne? [old kindness]." The unnamed pastor was probably trying to inspire his congregation by taking liberties with a familiar folk song that ended with the thought of always being happy to do God's work, no matter where that work sends you.

Several more songs using some of the lines now found in "Auld Lang Syne" surfaced over the next century, but it took a master scribe such as Burns to compose a version worth

Should auld acquaintance be
     forgot,
And never brought to mind?
Should auld acquaintance
     be forgot,
And auld lang syne?

Chorus:

For auld lang syne, my dear
For auld lang syne,
We'll tak a cup o kindness
     yet,
For auld lang syne!
And there's a hand my trusty
     fiere,
And gie's a hand o thine
And we'll tak a right guid-
     willie waught,
For auld lang syne.

Chorus

Translation

Should old acquaintance
     be forgotten
and never remembered
Should old acquaintance
     be forgotten
For old long ago

Chorus:

For old long ago, my dear
For old long ago
We will take a cup of
     kindness yet
For old long ago
And there is a hand my
     trusted friend
And give me a hand of yours
And we will take of a good
     drink/toast
For old long ago.

Chorus

remembering. Just before Christmas, in 1788, the great poet sent a letter to Frances Anna Dunlop. In the body of his correspondence, Burns wrote, "There is an old song and tune which has often thrilled through my soul. You know I am an enthusiast in old Scotch songs. I shall give you the verses on the other sheet." The song he sent was probably his initial draft of "Auld Lang Syne."

After several more rewrites, publisher James Johnson put Burns's poem, coupled with an old Scottish tune, in a 1796 edition of *Museum*. The melody, which the poet had suggested be used with the lyrics, had first been published in 1700. It was very well known and Burns himself had used it with at least two of his other poems. Ironically, though the poet knew Johnson was going to place "Auld Lang Syne" in the next issue of *Museum*, Burns never saw it. He died several months before his work would become well known in Great Britain.

Burns's song remained a number reserved for pubs and family reunions up until the time Lombardo played it in 1929. Yet even though it has become the national anthem of New Year's Eve, few Americans can sing more than just a few lines, and even fewer know what the lyrics to "Auld Lang Syne" actually mean. The reason for this is that few understand the Gaelic language. Still while its meaning often remains a mystery, the song somehow evokes warm emotions and conjures up sweet memories of people and places from long ago.

About three decades after Lombardo made "Auld Lang Syne" a New Year's Eve classic, songwriter Frank Military took another look at the old number. He felt it had unrealized potential and was determined to take it in a much different direction.

"It was my favorite song," Military explained. "I just thought I would stretch it a little."

By the time he decided to tackle rewriting "Auld Lang Syne," Military was already two decades into a hall of fame career of penning hits for Frank Sinatra, Tony Bennett, Rosemary Clooney, Andy Williams, and more than a hundred others. He was also a cutting-edge publisher and popular arranger.

"I called up Curtis Mann," Military recalled. "I had published a lot of his songs and had worked with him in the past. I told him about my idea of writing a Christmas version of 'Auld Lang Syne.' We got together in New York and finished it in about two days."

Military felt that the emotions that "Auld Lang Syne" evoked were perfect for Christmas. In his fertile mind, Christmas Eve, much more than New Year's Eve, was when families got together. On these occasions, old memories were relived and new ones were made. So using the old tune, he envisioned lyrics that celebrated Christ's birth as a "yuletide valentine." After all, there was no greater love in the history of the planet than what was realized on that first Christmas.

Military and Mann built on that theme of ultimate love and told a story of not just trees and toys but answered prayers. In their words the cheer was found not in a drink but in the spirits of those who knew the real meaning of the holiday. While touching quickly on the best of both secular and sacred Christmases, Military and Mann ended their very uplifting take on Burns's old song with the line:

> In sweet accord, to thank our Lord,
> For a Christmas auld lang syne.

Curtis Mann had already written some tunes for Bobby Darin. He knew the pop singer was looking for a Christmas song that would rival numbers like "Silver Bells" or "White Christmas." Mann and Military also knew something else: because of a heart condition Darin was living on borrowed time. The entertainer had made it clear he wanted to put a very spiritual stamp on some of his work during his brief time on earth.

When Bobby heard the demo, he smiled and said, "This is my 'White Christmas'!"

Bobby recorded "Christmas Auld Lang Syne" in 1960 when he was twenty-four years old. He released the song as a holiday offering along with his version of "Child of God." Darin would make "Christmas Auld Lang Syne" a standard at December concerts for the remainder of his life. Sadly, that was not very long. In 1973, at just thirty-seven, the pop singer passed away while undergoing open-heart surgery.

Immediately after Darin's death, few picked up on "Christmas Auld Lang Syne." It seemed that times had changed and inspirational holiday standards were not being embraced by the culture of the time. Yet fifteen years later, as people began to search for ways to put a deeper spiritual punch into the season, Bobby's holiday record began to hit holiday playlists again. Soon the Military-Mann song was also being used in major holiday production shows and had been incorporated into church musical presentations. Then a long list of major record artists, such as Gloria Estefan and Mark Anthony, placed it on their holiday albums. Finally, more than two decades after Frank Military was inspired to turn the New Year's anthem into a carol, "Christmas Auld Lang Syne" began to emerge as a holiday classic.

More than two hundred years ago Robert Burns reworked an old Scottish poem about love and friendship into a song that evoked a longing for days gone by. A century and a half later Guy Lombardo took Burns's song and made it a New Year's Eve tradition. Yet it would be Frank Military who would rework the lyrics again, shaping them back into a love song. This time the love was not limited by earthly bonds; rather the lyrics now embraced a spiritual love that started before time began, was realized in a manger, and will live on forever. Bobby Darin did not live to see it, but for millions his "Christmas Auld Lang

Syne" has come to mean more than "White Christmas" or "Silver Bells," because it not only proclaimed the joy found in the secular elements of the holiday but also acknowledged that the real reason for the season began "old long ago" in a humble manger in Bethlehem.

ACKNOWLEDGMENTS

A special thanks to:

Kathy Collins
Cindy Lambert
Autumn Miller
Angela Scheff
Joe Bonsell
Dwayne Allen
John Hillman
Rheda Jones
Lara Saggaese
Becky Boxberger
Stacey Martin
Jeralee Mathews

Read this excerpt from Ace Collins' next book,

STORIES BEHIND THE TRADITIONS
AND SONGS OF EASTER

(AT THE CROSS) ALAS, AND DID MY SAVIOR BLEED?

One of the most powerful Christian anthems ever written was penned three centuries ago by the father of English hymn writers. Yet in a sense, this familiar and dynamic Easter favorite, the song that played while America's own most revered composer of sacred music gave her heart to the Lord, remained unfinished for more than one hundred and fifty years. It wasn't until then that a veteran of the American Civil War provided an uplifting and personal spiritual coda to the hymn's inspired verses and transformed "Alas, and Did My Savior Bleed?" into "At the Cross." In the process, not only did the song's title change but its status as familiar closing hymn shifted to illustrious Easter anthem.

Few things about Isaac Watts' life were normal. As if foreshadowing the many challenges Isaac would face in his life, including long bouts of illness, Watts' father was confined to a dark, dank prison cell on the day Isaac was born, July 17, 1674. The elder Watts had earned his sentence because of his views of Christian worship, views that did not conform to the laws and traditions of the Church of England.

As church leaders would quickly find out, in the case of Isaac, the apple did not fall far from the tree. Even as a youth, Watts criticized the language of the psalms sung in Anglican worship. He labeled the psalms dull, convoluted, and lacking in contemporary meaning. Isaac's father, both proud of and bemused by his son's views, challenged Isaac to "do better." He urged him to create new music which better reflected New Testament faith.

Over the next fifty years, Isaac would meet this challenge by composing more than six hundred hymns and becoming the best-known writer of sacred songs in the world. In a very real sense, he revolutionized Christian music, thereby opening the door to new thinking about every facet of church worship. Remarkably, when Watts composed his hymns, he thought not so much as a musician as a Bible student. Therefore his theologically sound musical messages not only reached his generation but also have continued to inspire each new generation of Christians in ways that few other songwriters ever have. Even today it is hard to imagine a worship service that does not owe something to Watts.

Watts was driven as few have ever been to fully understand every facet of his faith. As a teen, Isaac was denied admittance into any major English college because he was not a member of the Church of England. The obviously gifted Watts therefore received his formal schooling at lesser-known private academies. Yet this not did hold the lad back. Watts often spent days without sleep or exercise while studying the Bible, as well as all the theological books he could lay his hands on. He marked those volumes, wrote notes in the margins, and composed papers challenging long-accepted ideas. Before he reached his twentieth birthday, he had become one of England's most eloquent biblical scholars. By the age of twenty-four, he began a career as a pastor that would quickly bring him recognition as one of the most esteemed church leaders of the Calvinist movement. This

Alas, and did my Savior bleed,
And did my Sov'reign die?
Would He devote that sacred head
For such a worm as I?
Thy body slain, sweet Jesus, thine,
And bathed in its own blood,
While all exposed to wrath divine
The glorious Suff'rer stood!
Was it for crimes that I had done
He groaned upon the tree?
Amazing pity! grace unknown!
And love beyond degree!
Well might the sun in darkness hide,
And shut his glories in,
When God, the mighty Maker, died
For man, the creature's sin.

Thus might I hide my blushing face
While his dear cross appears,
Dissolve my heart in thankfulness,
And melt mine eyes to tears.
But drops of grief can ne'er repay
The debt of love I owe;
Here, Lord, I give myself away,
'Tis all that I can do.

Chorus:
At the cross, at the cross
Where I first saw the light,
And the burden of my heart rolled away,
It was there by faith
I received my sight,
And now I am happy all the day.

in spite of the fact that his frail health often left him bedridden for months at a time.

Because he was a theologian first, Watts viewed music in terms of biblical constraints. He framed his songs within the confines of the true nature of Christ's life on earth and his death on the cross. So when Isaac took himself back in time to "view" the crucifixion, it was natural that he so immersed himself in this study that it was as if he were seeing it with his own eyes. To accomplish this perspective, Watts pored over historical documents that fully described a Roman crucifixion. What he uncovered both overwhelmed and revolted him. As he reread the scriptural accounts of Good Friday, he became so humbled by his new understanding of the suffering that Jesus endured for sinners that he felt moved to write about it in graphic terms.

On that day in 1707 when Watts penned his newest hymn, he broke open a fresh way of looking at the events of Easter. Never before had the pain of Christ's death been painted with such descriptive passion. It was in a sense horrifying. The imagery in the second verse of "Alas, and Did My Savior Bleed?" fully reflects the writer's awe of the price paid by his Lord. In Watts' mind and in his words, this was anything but a pretty picture. Perhaps that is why this verse is rarely found in hymnals today:

> Thy body slain, sweet Jesus, thine,
> And bathed in its own blood,
> While all exposed to wrath divine
> The glorious Suff'rer stood!

The other unique and explicit element of this spiritual standard that is often changed today is the line "for such a worm as I." Modern men and women simply don't like to see themselves in this light. Watts knew that compared with the majesty and power of Christ, he had little more worth than that of a mindless creature who dug through the dirt. And yet realizing that Jesus loved him enough to die for him made the cross a symbol not just of agonizing death but also of great hope and love.

When published in 1707, "Alas, and Did My Savior Bleed?" quickly became more than an Easter hymn. It was one of the most used songs in the hymnals of the day. For more than 170 years, at most Protestant worship services, this Watts' classic would be the historical equivalent of "Just As I Am." It was employed almost exclusively as an invitation call. As such, it would have a profound effect on American Christian music. The power of Watts' work might best be seen in the conversion testimony of the mother of American hymn writers.

In 1850, a thirty-year-old blind woman found herself at a church service. This fragile sinner was moved by the message she heard that day, but she didn't feel the urge to acknowledge her faith until the invitation hymn was played. When Fanny Crosby heard "Alas, and Did My Savior Bleed?" she took special note of Watts' description of the Christ dying on the cross. Crosby would later tell her friends, "When they sang the lyric, 'Here, Lord, I give myself away — 'tis all that I can do,' then I had to yield to the call. My very soul flooded with celestial light. I sprang to my feet, shouting 'Hallelujah.'"

Thanks in no small part to the dynamic message of Watts' hymn, Fanny Crosby composed hundreds of sacred favorites, including "To God Be the Glory," "Jesus Is Tenderly Calling," "Blessed Assurance," "Rescue the Perishing," and "Tell Me the Story of Jesus." Yet as Crosby lived her incredible life, it was the Watts hymn that seemed to continue to be the model for her own Christian service.

Ralph Hudson had been a Union soldier in the Civil War. He served for three long years and survived some of the bloodiest battles in the fight to preserve the United States. He not only felt blessed to escape the war with his health but was moved to use the remainder of his life in service to the God who had seen him through those many battles. In the days after the war, Hudson would tell his friends, "I have been saved for something." And he began looking for it.

At Ohio's Mount Union College, Hudson taught music during the week and spent his weekends telling the story of God's grace in pulpits. He also found time to compose more than forty hymns. Like Fanny Crosby, Hudson was continually drawn to the Watts' standard, "Alas, and Did My Savior Bleed?" Yet unlike any before who had studied the classic hymn, the music teacher felt it was not complete. It needed something. Yes, Hudson acknowledged, Watts had written a powerful vision of Christ's suffering on the cross, while clearly painting a haunting verbal image of the debt that all Christians owed Christ, but he believed that the message needed to end with the uplifting hope found in the resurrection. So in very simple language, set to music that was much more elementary and different in tone and tempo from that of the original hymn, Hudson added the reason Christians were drawn to the cross; he described the real hope found in Easter itself.

> At the cross, at the cross
> Where I first saw the light,
> And the burden of my heart rolled away,
> It was there by faith
> I received my sight,
> And now I am happy all the day.

At first glance, the chorus and verses don't seem to go together. Yet when they're sung, it's obvious they do complement each other. The haunting melody of the verses sets up the triumphant response of those who find the living Christ by taking another look at the meaning of a cross that could not stop his mission or his life.

By the early 1900s, Hudson's chorus had largely been accepted as a vital part of Watts' lyrics. With this musical marriage, "At the Cross" became one of the most beloved hymns used in Easter services around the world.

If he had lived in Hudson's day, Isaac Watts probably would have enthusiastically sung Ralph Hudson's chorus. It was his nature to look at the hopeful side of faith with words that touched the heart rather than entranced the mind. He once told a congregation that his views on spreading the message were much different from those of most pastors. "I hate the thought of making anything in religion heavy or tiresome," Watts explained. "Suppose two preachers were desired to minister to the same subject. One of them has all the beauty, force, and skill of clear and calm reasoning; the other not only instructs well, but powerfully moves the affections with sacred oratory. Which of these two will best secure the attention of the people, and guard them from drowsiness or wandering? Surely, he that touches the heart will fix the eyes and the ears and all the powers; while he that merely endeavors to inform the head will find many wandering eyes, and some sleepers."

It took both Watts and Hudson to write one of the most moving of all Easter hymns, to give it the power to touch the soul. One composer told the Easter story in stark imagery, while the other delivered the message of hope found at the cross in language even a child could understand. Together, these two brought Christ's death and resurrection to life in a timeless manner that still leads sinners home and leaves believers awestruck.

Stories Behind the Best-Loved Songs of Christmas

Ace Collins

Behind the Christmas songs we love to sing lie fascinating stories that will enrich your holiday celebration. Taking you inside the nativity of over thirty favorite songs and carols, Ace Collins introduces you to people you've never met, stories you've never heard, and meanings you'd never have imagined.

The next time you and your family sing "God Rest Ye Merry Gentlemen," you'll have a new understanding of its message and popular roots. You'll learn the strange history of the haunting and powerful "O Holy Night." And you'll step inside the life of Mark Lowry and find out how he came to pen the words to the contemporary classic "Mary, Did You Know?"

Joining hands with such modern favorites as "White Christmas" and "The Christmas Song," they are part of the legacy of inspiration, faith, tears, love, and spiritual joy that is Christmas.

From the rollicking appeal of "Jingle Bells" to the tranquil beauty of "Silent Night," the great songs of Christmas contain messages of peace, hope, and truth. Each in its own way expresses a facet of God's heart and celebrates the birth of his greatest gift to the world—Jesus, the most wonderful Christmas Song of all.

Hardcover, Jacketed: 0-310-23926-5

Stories Behind the Great Traditions of Christmas

Ace Collins

The golden traditions of Christmas—gifts, wreaths, stockings, carols, mistletoe, and more—infuse our celebration of the season with meaning and glowing memories. And, in ways you may not realize, they point us to the birth of Christ.

Stories Behind the Great Traditions of Christmas reveals the people, places, and events that shaped the best-loved customs of this merriest of holidays. Here are spiritual insights, true-life tales, and captivating legends to intrigue you and your family and bring new luster and depth to your celebration of Jesus' birth. Discover how

- after eighteen centuries of all but ignoring the event, churches began to open the door for believers to commemorate Jesus' incarnation.
- the evergreen tree, once a central theme in the worship practices of pagan cultures, came to represent the everlasting love of God.
- the magi's three gifts—gold, frankincense, and myrrh—are filled with spiritual symbolism.

The stories in this book will warm your heart as you rediscover the true and eternal significance of Christmas.

Hardcover, Jacketed: 0-310-24880-9

Stories Behind the Hymns That Inspire America
Songs That Unite Our Nation

Ace Collins

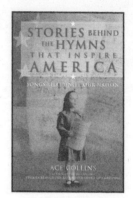

From the moment the pilgrims landed on the shores of the New World, to the dark days following September 11th, songs of faith have inspired, comforted, and rallied our beloved country. *Stories Behind the Hymns That Inspire America* describes the people, places, and events that have shaped the heart and soul of America. The stories behind these songs will fascinate you and bring new meaning and richness to special spiritual moments in the history of our nation.

The songs in this book have energized movements, illuminated dark paths, commemorated historic events, taken the message of freedom and faith across this nation and beyond, healed broken spirits, and righted wrongs. Their stories will make you proud of your heritage as you realize anew that in America, even one voice can have a lasting influence.

Hardcover, Jacketed 0-310-24879-5

Turn Your Radio On

The Stories Behind Gospel Music's All-Time Greatest Songs

Ace Collins

Turn Your Radio On tells the fascinating stories behind gospel music's most unforgettable songs, including "Amazing Grace," "The Battle Hymn of the Republic," "He Touched Me," "I'll Fly Away," "Were You There?" and many more. These are the songs that have shaped our faith and brought us joy.

You'll find out what famous song traces back to a sailor's desperate prayer, what Bill Gaither tune was recorded by Elvis Presley in 1969—and won a Grammy—and what song was born during a carriage ride through Washington, D.C., at the onset of the Civil War. *Turn Your Radio On* is an inspiring journey through the songs that are part of the roots of our faith today.

Softcover: 0-310-21153-0

ZONDERVAN®

GRAND RAPIDS, MICHIGAN 49530 USA

WWW.ZONDERVAN.COM

I Saw Him in Your Eyes

Everyday People Making
Extraordinary Impact in the
Lives of Karen Kingsbury, Terri
Blackstock, Bobby Bowden,
Charlie Daniels, S. Truett Cathy,
and More.

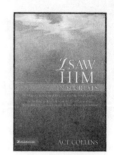

Ace Collins

This collection of moving stories reveals the power of
ordinary people to shape the lives of others in unexpected, sometimes astonishing ways. Bestselling author
Ace Collins presents the inspiring recollections of some
of America's best-loved leaders. These uplifting personal
accounts reveal the life-changing impact of a simple kind
act, of a good word spoken at the right time, of an everyday life whose unassuming character makes all the difference in someone else's world.

These and other real-life stories will encourage you,
uplift you, and fill you with gratitude for those who have
touched your own life. And they will cause you to consider your purpose and potential. Today may be the day
when your own ordinary life influences someone else in
an extraordinary way.

Softcover: 0-310-26318-2

The Cathedrals

The Story of America's Best-Loved
Gospel Quartet

*From the founding members
Glen Payne and George Younce
with Ace Collins*

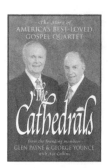

For more than thirty years the Cathedrals, America's most popular male quartet, have told the gospel in song from London to New York, from the Holy Land to Nashville. They have appeared on *The Today Show*, *Prime Time Country*, and almost every Bill Gaither "Old Friends" special. They have sung with orchestras and renowned choirs, and opened up southern gospel music to millions who had never heard it before they heard the Cathedrals.

The Cathedrals tells the inside story of this beloved gospel group and the two men whose voices have helped make it famous. From early struggles on the road to the heights of popularity, here's the heartwarming, firsthand account of their amazing success and longevity. Scores of black-and-white and color photos chronicle changes over the years, while lyrics from the most popular songs show you why the music of the Cathedrals has charmed audiences for more than three decades.

A must-have for any fan of southern gospel music or those who love a stirring and inspirational biography.

Softcover: 0-310-23520-0

We want to hear from you. Please send your comments about this book to us in care of zreview@zondervan.com. Thank you.

GRAND RAPIDS, MICHIGAN 49530 USA

ZONDERVAN.COM/
AUTHORTRACKER